READY TO PAINT

Irises in Watercolour

Julie King

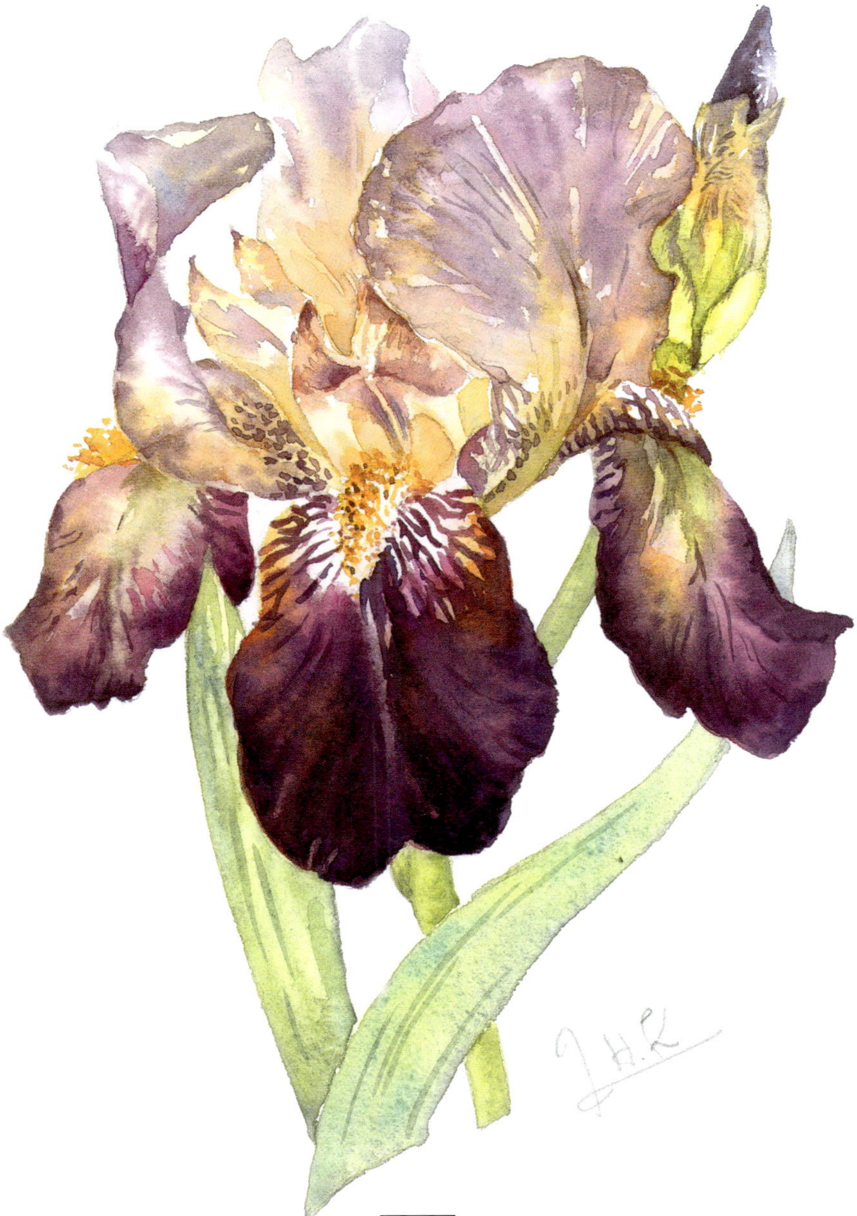

SEARCH PRESS

First published in Great Britain 2012

Search Press Limited
Wellwood, North Farm Road,
Tunbridge Wells, Kent TN2 3DR

Photographs by Debbie Patterson at Search Press Studios

ISBN: 978-1-84448-721-9

Suppliers
If you have any difficulty obtaining any of the materials and equipment mentioned in this book, please visit the Search Press website: www.searchpress.com

Publishers' notes
All the step-by-step photographs in this book feature the author, Julie King, demonstrating her watercolour painting techniques. No models have been used.

Please note: when removing the perforated sheets of tracing paper from the book, score them first, then carefully pull out each sheet.

Share your Ready to Paint artworks with the world. Simply go to the 'Ready to Paint' page on Facebook and upload your images.

Printed in China

Dedication

I dedicate this book to my mother Janet and my late father Robert Conway King.

Acknowledgements

Many thanks to everyone at Search Press, particularly my editor Alison Shaw and photographer Debbie Patterson; both a pleasure to work with. Thank you to all my students, friends and family for your continued support and encouragement and for providing me with flowers from your gardens!

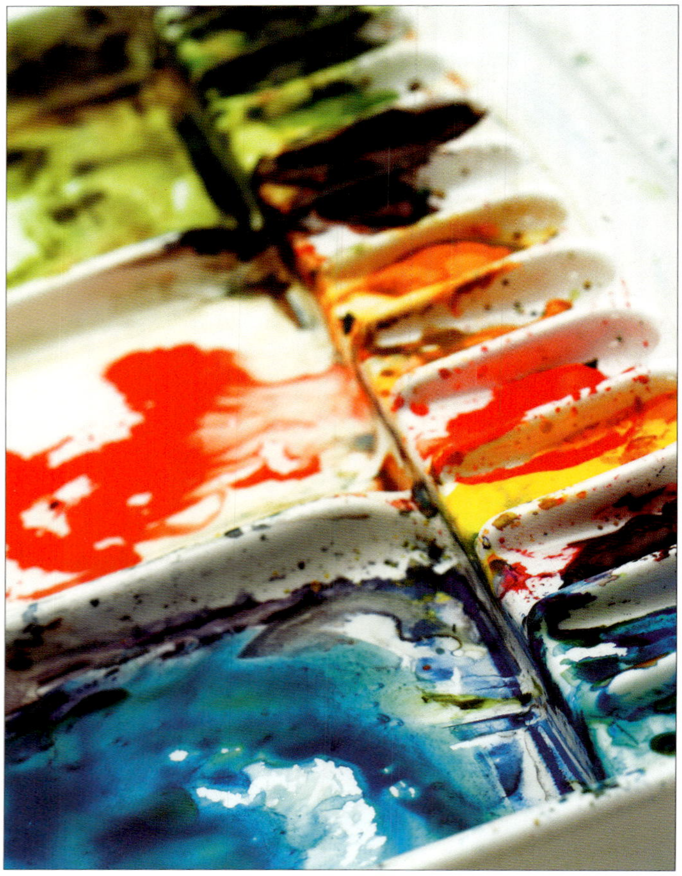

Page 1

Bearded Iris
23 x 30.5cm (9 x 12in)
A beautiful richly-coloured iris, with velvety lower petals which contrast with the soft delicate upper petals.

Opposite

Siberian Irises
44 x 30.5cm (17¼ x 12in)
Often found growing at the waterside, these elegant irises provide a tall, vertical composition, enhanced by their narrow, lance-shaped foliage.

Contents

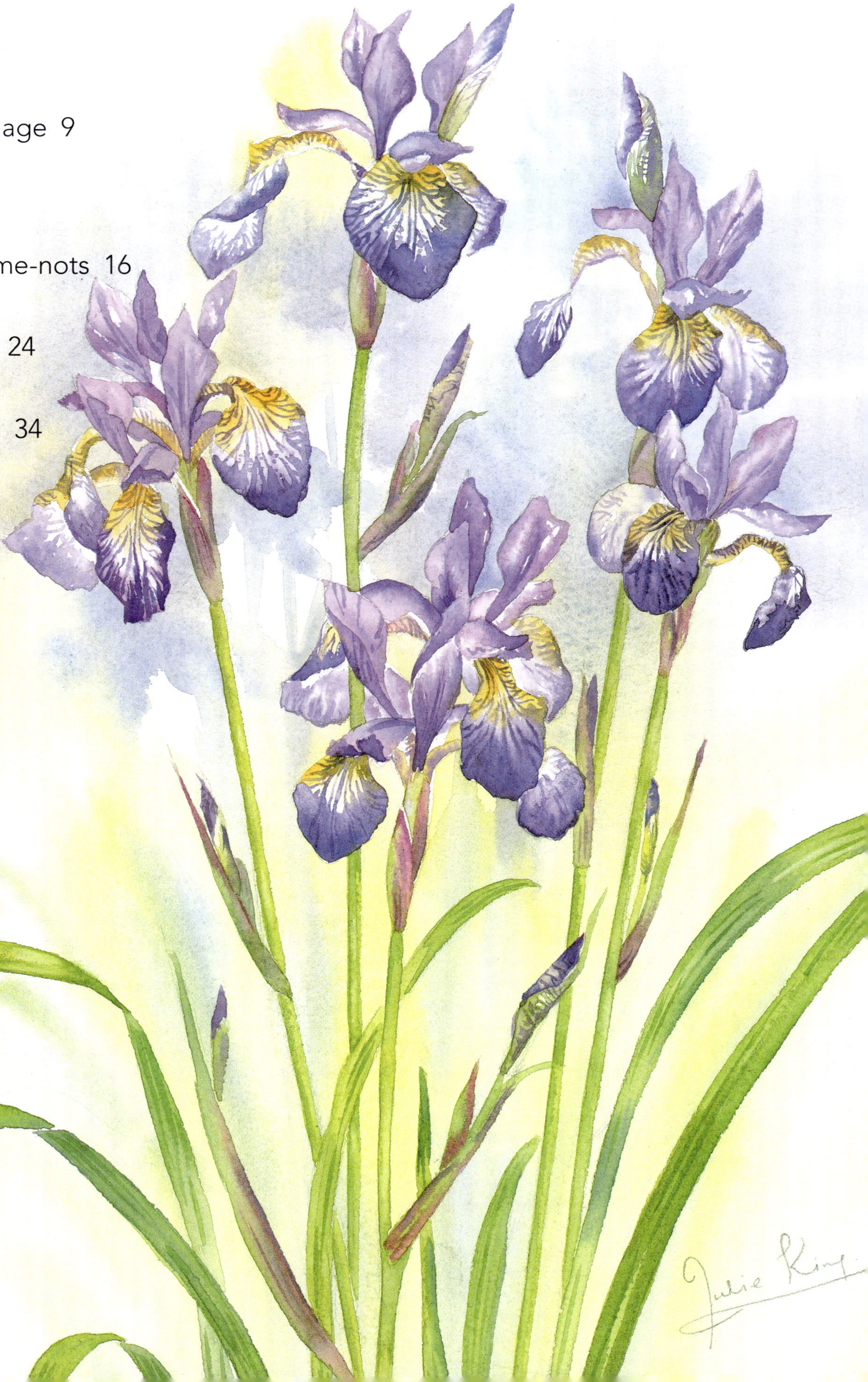

Introduction

Irises have always been one of my favourite flowers so I was delighted to be asked to demonstrate my method of painting them in this book.

Irises bring a garden to life, with their colours and form. They are full of life and movement and are most amazing in their construction. Their flower heads are made up of three upright petals and three falling petals which appear to drape like a fabric with a strong central vein. Their leaves are equally distinctive, having a blade or sword-like appearance.

The word 'iris' is of Greek origin, meaning 'rainbow' or 'colourful', and irises certainly grow in many colours: blue, purple, pink, orange, red, yellow, white and even black.

It is a popular plant which has featured in the work of many prolific artists over the years, including Vincent Van Gogh, Claude Monet and Georgia O'Keeffe.

The aim of this book is to give you inspiration and guidance to paint irises in watercolour. In order for you to concentrate on the techniques of painting without being overwhelmed with the drawing, I have pre-prepared a selection of iris paintings and produced them as line drawings. Six tracings have been attached to the front of the book which can be removed and transferred to your paper (instructions shown). I have demonstrated how to translate five of the tracings into beautiful paintings, capturing the essence of an iris to include a variety of specimens, colours, techniques and backgrounds.

I prepared my paintings in the spring and early summer time, sketching and painting directly from the flowers, either in situ, or to make it easier, cutting and bringing the irises into the studio to study. I also took reference photographs, as once they are picked, the life of each bloom is quite short.

Watercolour is a very spontaneous, flowing medium so don't worry if your painting is not exactly the same as mine. No repeated painting is identical!

Following my guidance and tips, use this book as a learning exercise and in no time I am sure you will be inspired to create beautiful paintings of the irises in your own garden.

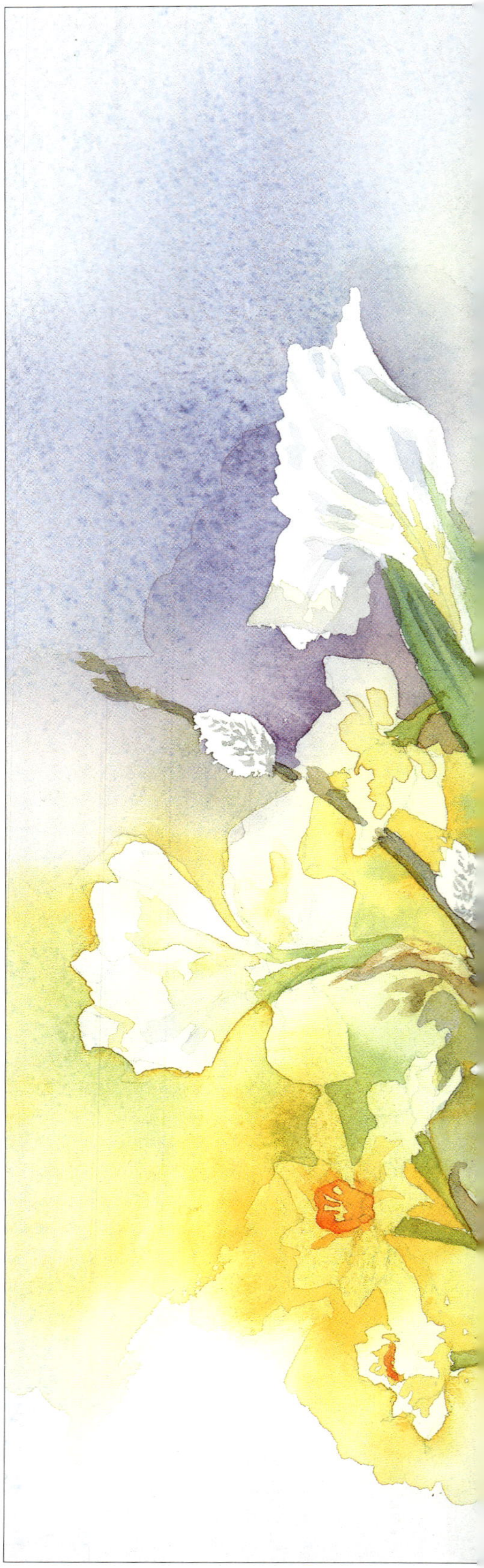

TRACING 6

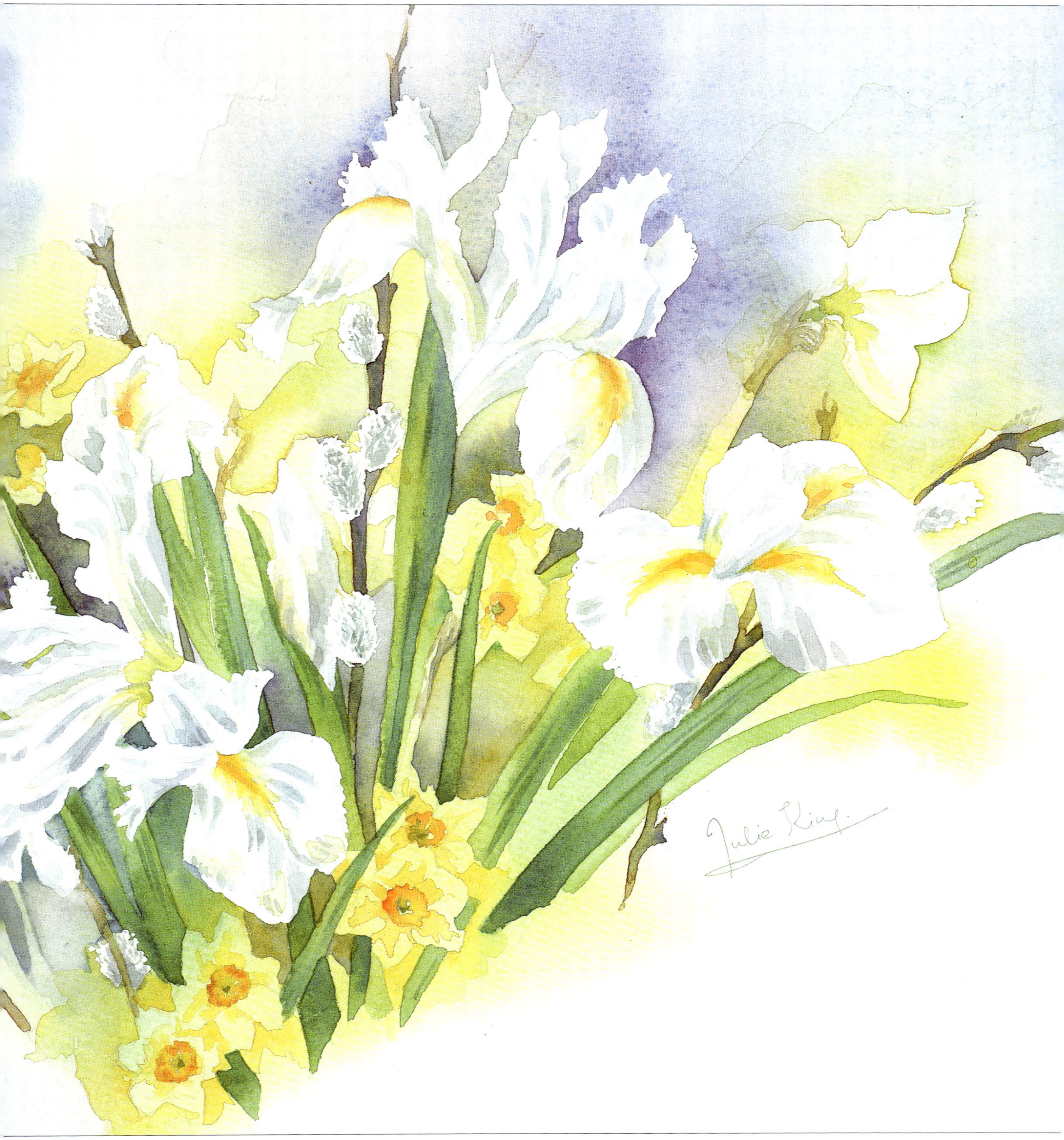

Springtime

45.5 x 30.5cm (18 x 12in)

I bought a bunch of white irises and combined them with daffodils and pussy willow to create an arrangement in the studio. The yellow flowers create a contrasting background to the white of the irises, and to add more life to the arrangement I introduced a complementary purple shade. When you have completed the five demonstrations, have a go at painting this composition, which incorporates the techniques covered. The bonus tracing 6 is provided for you.

Materials

Paints

Watercolour paints are available in both tubes and half or full pans, which are solid blocks of colour. Both are suitable for painting flowers. My personal preference is for pans in either a metal or plastic palette as the colours are immediately accessible and ideal for both studio and outdoor work.

There are two types of paint, student quality and artists' quality. Student quality is quite adequate to start with; however, if you can afford the more expensive artists' quality, you will find that the pigments are superior. Due to the intensity of the pigment, less paint is required when mixing and the results are clean and fresh.

I have used a variety of colours in the following projects based around the three primary colours, red, blue and yellow and have selected shades varying from cool to warm.

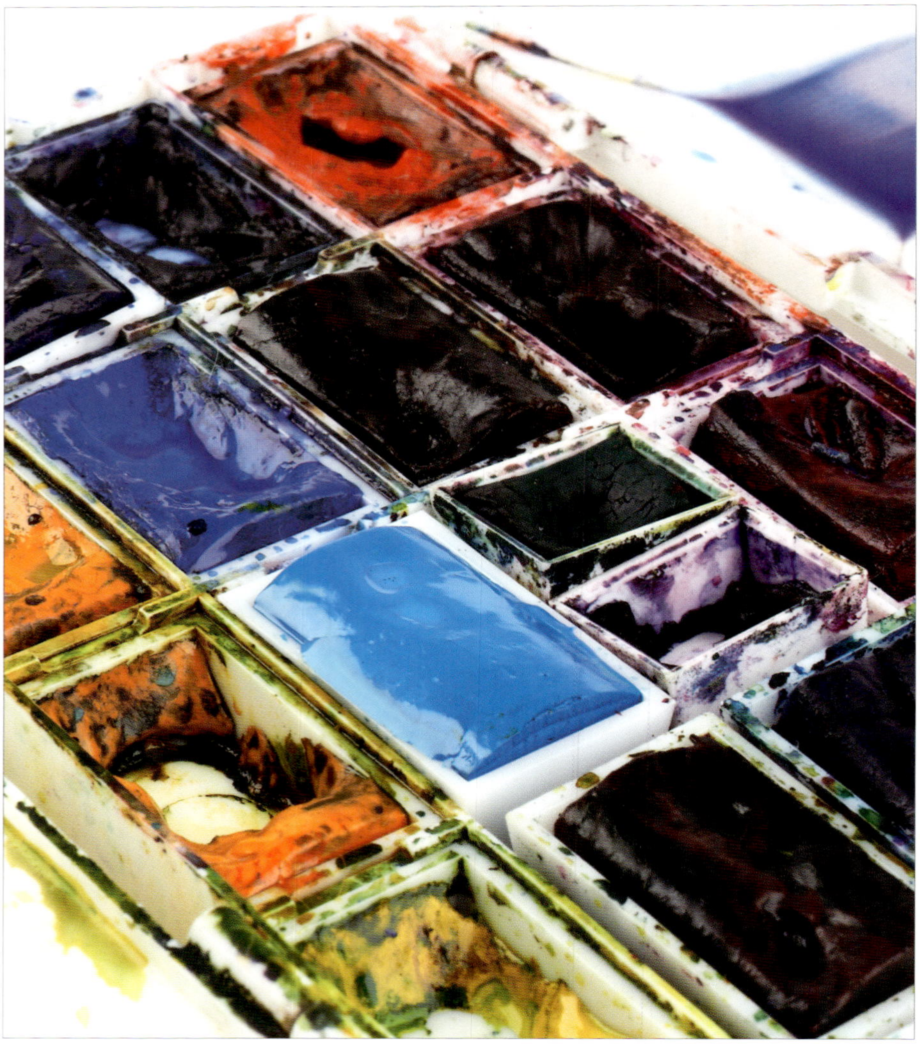

A typical watercolour artist's palette, made up of pans of watercolour paint.

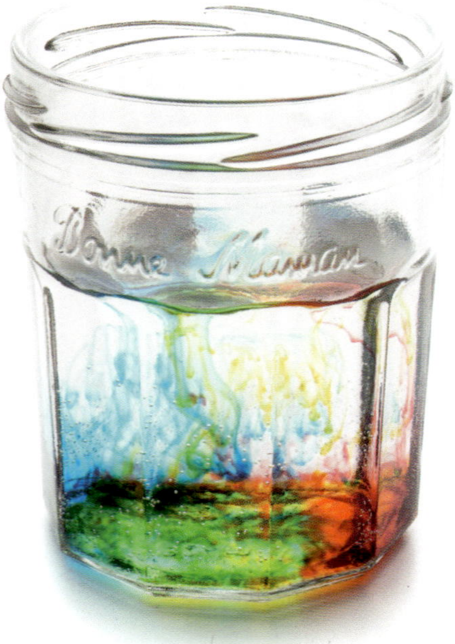

The palette is as follows:

Red/pink: quinacridone magenta, permanent rose, alizarin crimson.

Blue: cerulean blue, Winsor blue (green shade) cobalt blue, French ultramarine and indigo.

Yellow: aureolin, new gamboge, Indian yellow and raw sienna.

To this range I have also added sap green and burnt sienna.

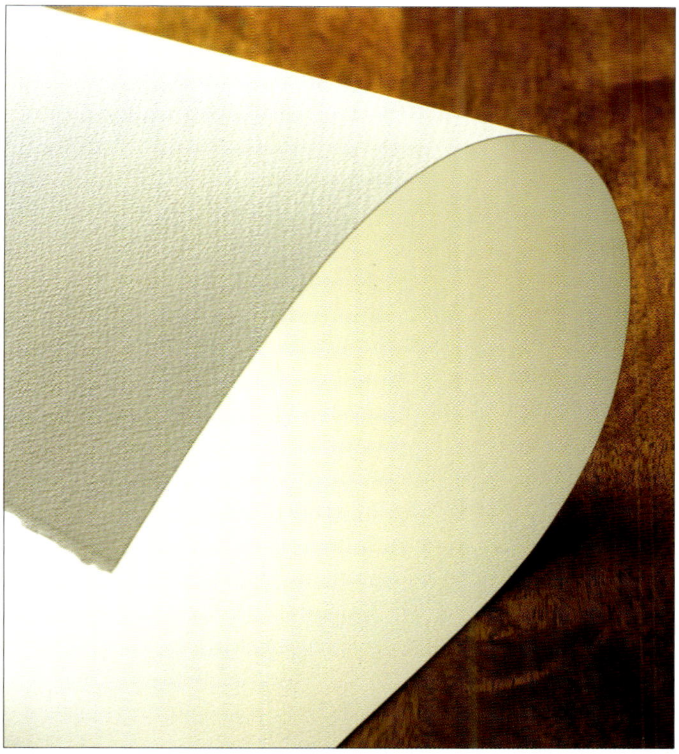

300gsm (140lb) Not paper, suitable for all the projects in this book.

Paper

Watercolour paper is available in a variety of weights and finishes. Weights vary from a lightweight, thinner paper of 185gsm (90lb), which generally requires stretching to prevent the paper buckling, to a heavyweight thick paper of 640gsm (300lb). I recommend, and generally use a mid-weight 300gsm (140lb) paper. It is versatile and thick enough for most purposes without having to stretch it.

There are three choices of paper surface: (HP) hot pressed which is smooth and good for fine detail, (Not) cold pressed with a medium texture, ideal for every subject and technique, and finally, Rough, a very textured paper.

Paper is available to purchase in large sheets, pads or blocks.

Brushes

In my demonstrations I have used round brushes, in sizes 4, 5, 8, 10 and 12. I tend to favour sable brushes as they hold plenty of paint and retain their point, enabling you to make fine strokes as well as broader washes. A good quality nylon brush is a good and less expensive alternative providing it retains a good point. In addition I use a cheap or old brush for applying masking fluid.

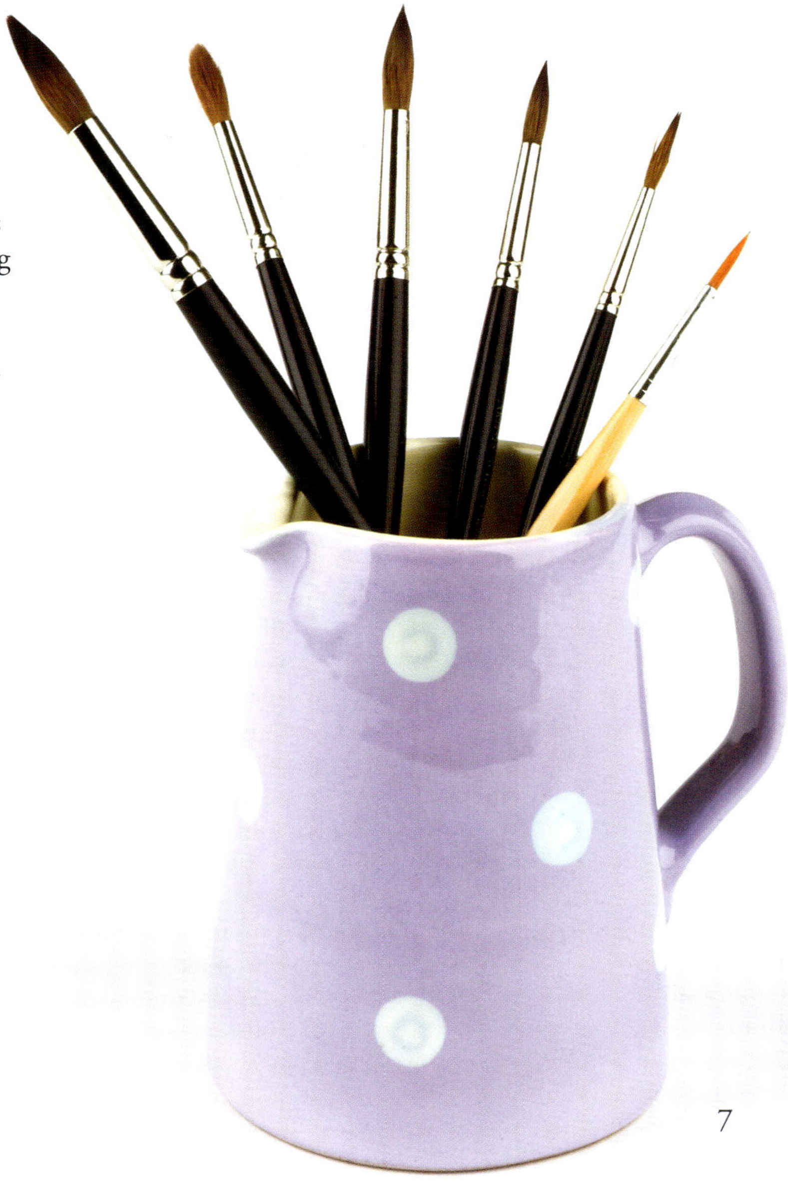

A selection of brushes used in this book.

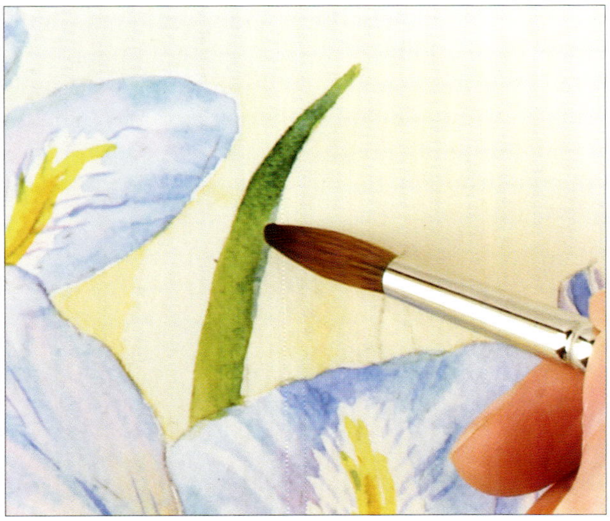

Other materials

H and 2B pencils A hard and soft pencil is required for transferring the image to watercolour paper.

Eraser This is used to remove any pencil lines that are still visible when the painting is complete.

Pencil sharpener When transferring the image the pencils need a good, sharp point.

Masking tape This will be needed when transferring the image and also for securing the watercolour paper on to a board.

Sheet of cartridge paper Provides a bright, white surface on which to prepare the tracing.

Kitchen paper I often lean on a sheet of folded paper whilst painting, and I frequently use it to absorb excess paint or water from my brush and to quickly freshen up my palette.

Palette A palette with wells and a good mixing area is essential for preparing your colours.

Water pots I recommend using two water pots: one for rinsing your brushes and one clean jar to use for re-wetting areas on your painting.

Masking fluid A solution used to mask off areas of a painting to retain the whiteness of the paper.

Old/cheap brush Use this to apply the masking fluid. To help protect the brush, dip it into soapy water before using the masking fluid.

Hairdryer You can use a hairdryer to speed up the drying process.

Wooden board Whether you are working on a single sheet of paper, a block or a pad, a wooden board provides a support which can be tilted slightly at an angle and moved around if necessary.

Clockwise from top left: water pot, masking tape, hairdryer, masking fluid, palette, eraser, pencils, pencil sharpener, kitchen paper and reference photograph.

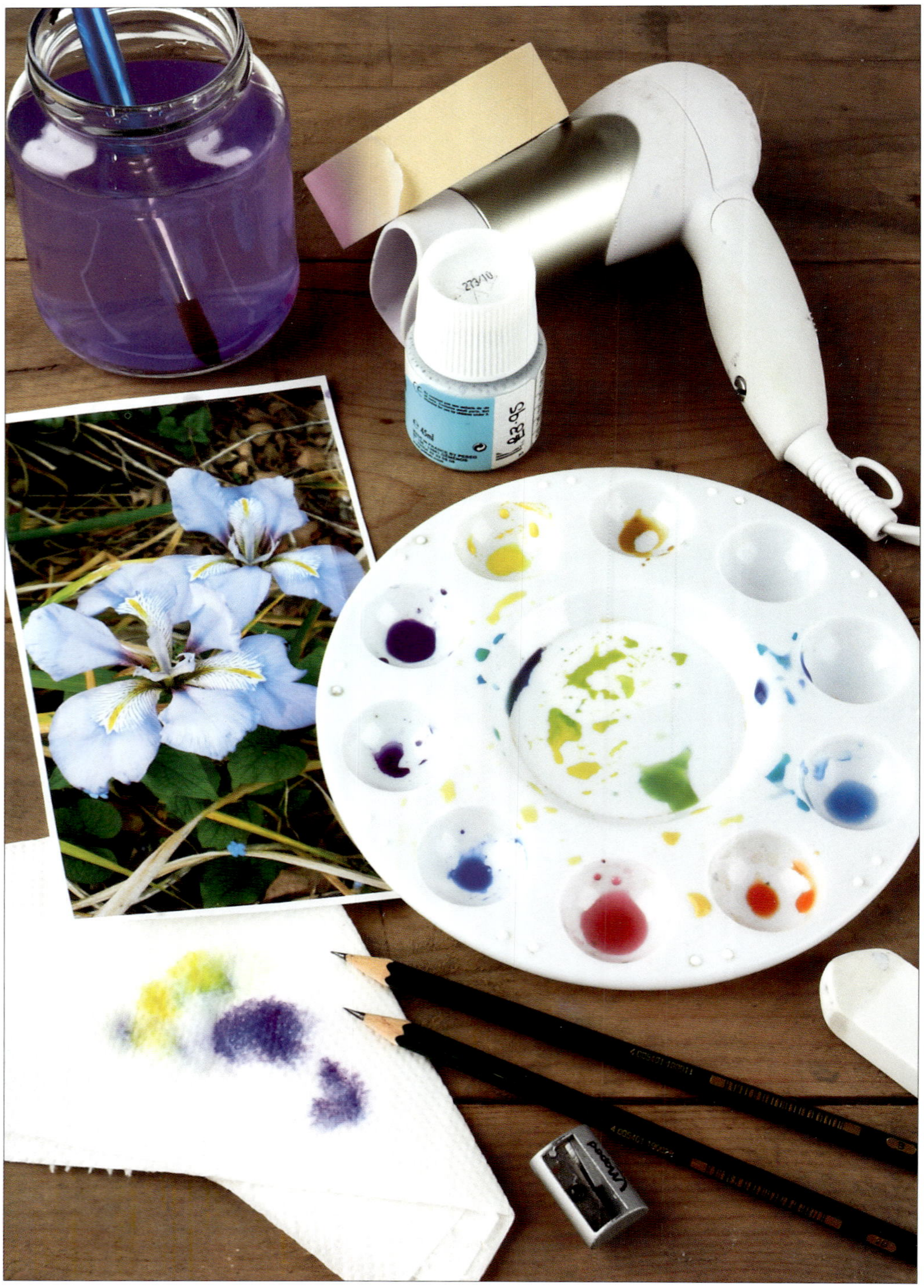

Transferring the image

Tracings of each project are provided at the front of the book, and there is a bonus tracing for the painting on pages 4–5. Carefully remove the tracing of your choice and follow the instructions shown below to transfer the image to watercolour paper.

The tracings can be reused several times, enabling you to create different versions.

Tip

To avoid smudging the lines, always have a folded piece of kitchen paper for resting your hand on, and keep your pencil sharpened to a fine point.

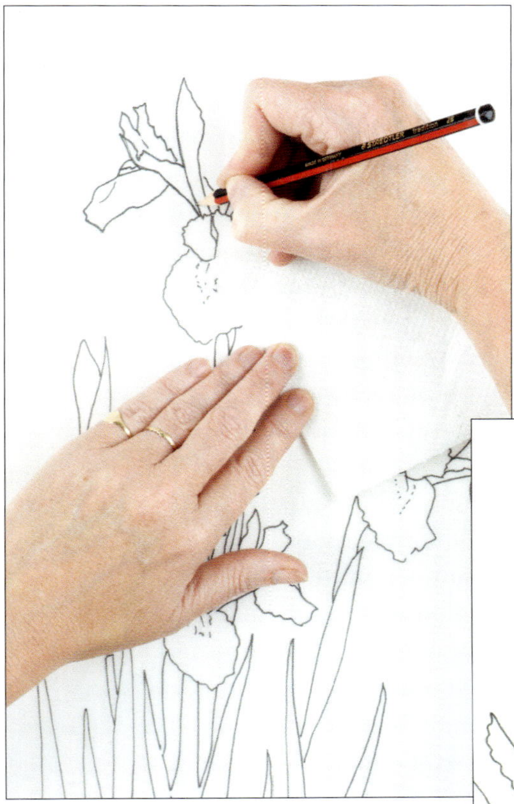

1 Reverse the tracing. Tape it down on to a separate sheet of white cartridge paper. Use a 2B pencil and go over each line.

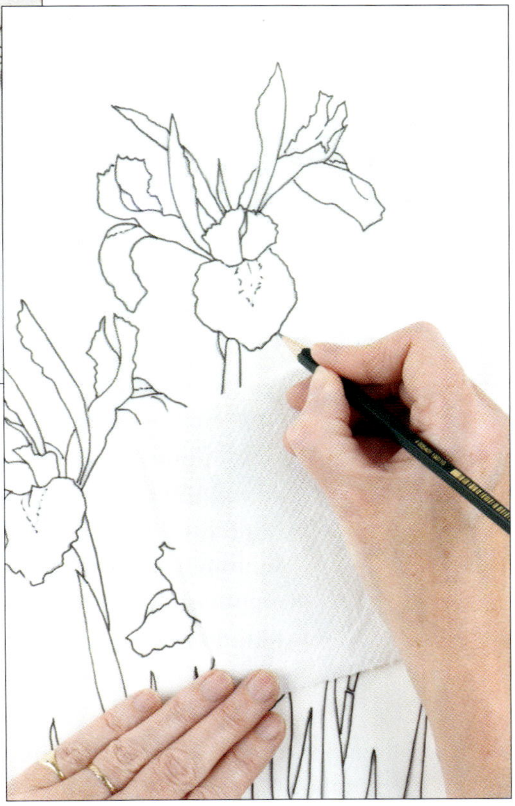

2 Turn the tracing over to the correct side and tape it to a sheet of watercolour paper. Using a hard pencil, such as an H, go over each line again. Alternatively, use a spoon handle and rub gently over each line.

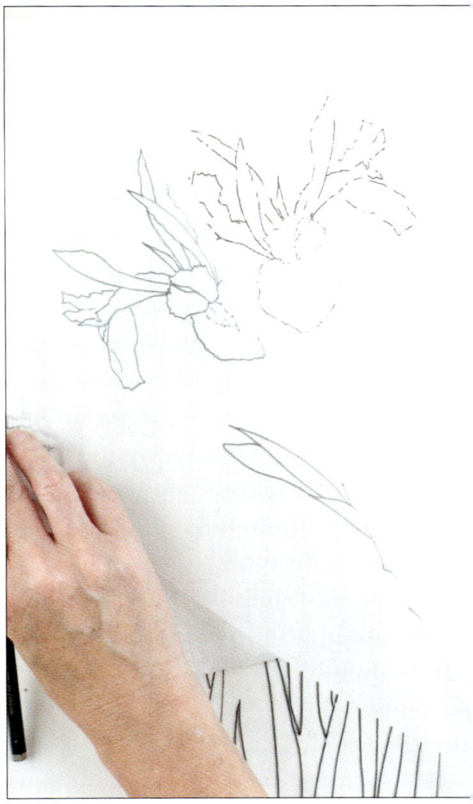

3 Lift up the tracing to reveal the image transferred on to the watercolour paper, ready for you to begin painting.

Dutch Irises

TRACING
1

These purple irises create a stunning, yet simple composition on a crisp, white background, accentuating their height, sword-shaped leaves and the beautiful elegant structure of each flower head. The three components of this type of flower head are clearly visible: the larger rich purple lower petals, the frilly petals and the elongated slender petals stretching upwards.

You will need

300gsm (140lb) Not watercolour paper

Colours: aureolin, new gamboge, cerulean blue, French ultramarine, permanent rose

Brushes: size 5 round, size 8 round

Pencils: 2B, H

Kitchen paper

Eraser

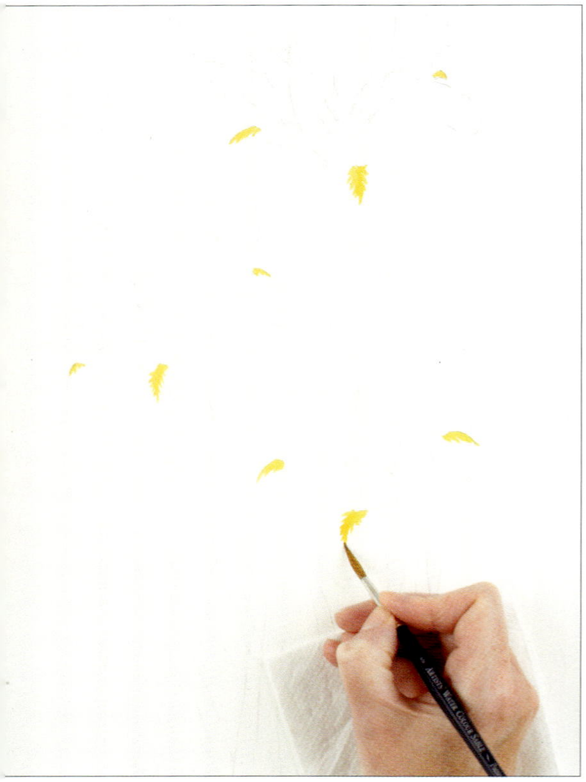

Tip

Wash your hands before starting to paint!

1 Transfer the image to the paper following the instructions on page 9. Make a pool of strong new gamboge with a little water and apply the colour wet-on-dry with a size 5 round brush on each lower petal. Draw your brush from the top of the petal downwards and sweep it out to either side.

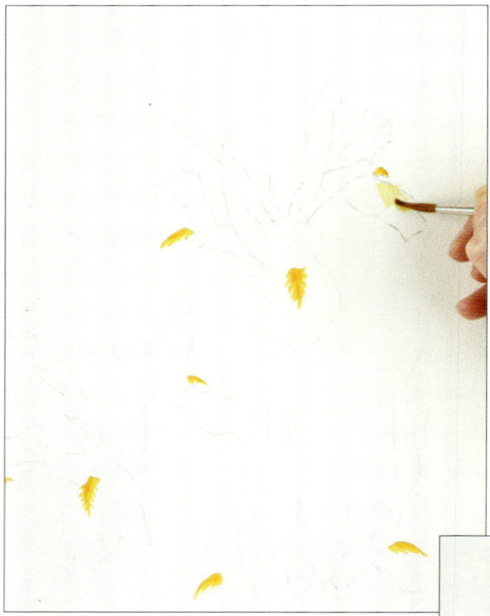

2 Dilute the new gamboge and place a touch of this light yellow on the underside of the petals, where it is needed – on the top-right underside petal and the lower-left petal on the iris to its side. Allow to dry.

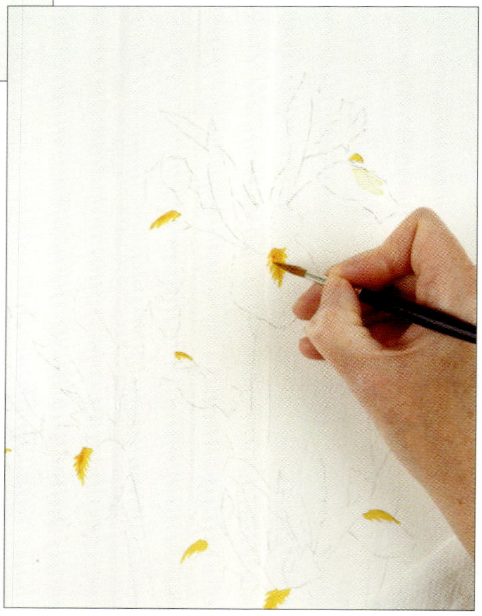

3 Add a touch of permanent rose to the new gamboge to make a warmer and stronger shade. Apply wet-on-dry over the base yellow by sweeping the brushstrokes downwards. Let the colours dry.

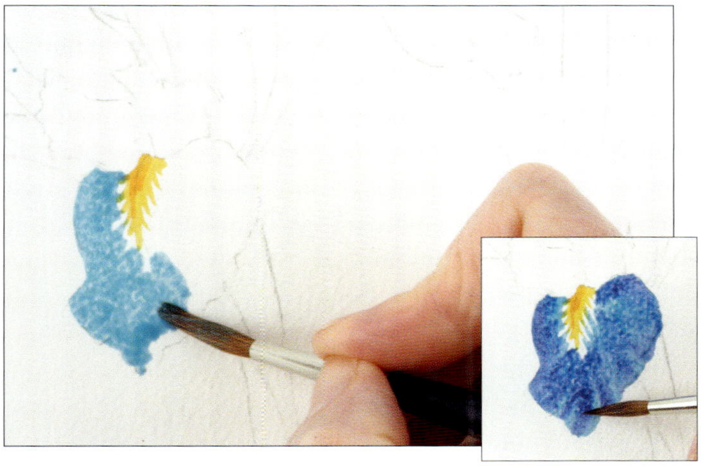

4 Mix three washes: a cerulean blue; a blue-purple mix: French ultramarine and a touch of permanent rose; a pink-purple mix: permanent rose with a touch of French ultramarine. Continuing with the size 5 brush, apply the cerulean wash on to the lower petal, working wet-on-dry, leaving a gap around the yellow. The cerulean blue granulates to create an effective texture, especially when combined with other colours. While this is wet, drop in the pink-purple mix, using the point of the brush, working from the outside inwards.

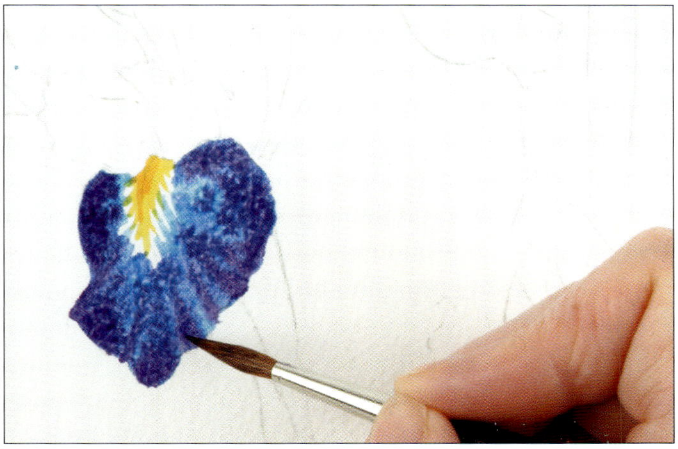

5 Continuing wet-in-wet, add more depth by applying the deeper blue-purple mix, stippling and brushing in the colour with the point of the brush towards the centre to suggest the deeper shadows.

Tip

If you have to create more washes, don't worry about varying the colour a little. This adds to the natural look of the flower.

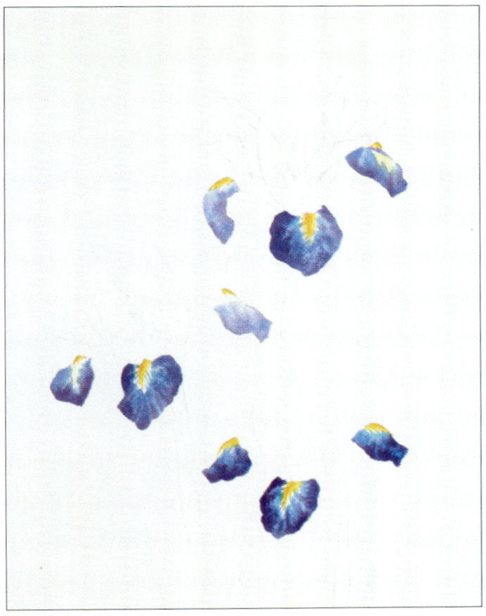

6 Complete the petals, varying the strength of colour on them; the undersides can be a little paler.

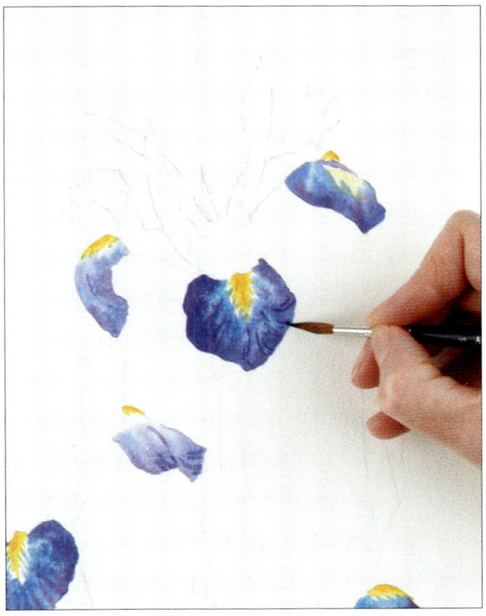

7 Paint in the veins using a French ultramarine and permanent rose mid-tone wash on the lighter petals, and a stronger mix, using less water, of the same two colours on the darker petals. Draw the point of the brush from the edge inwards. This helps give more movement and form to the petals.

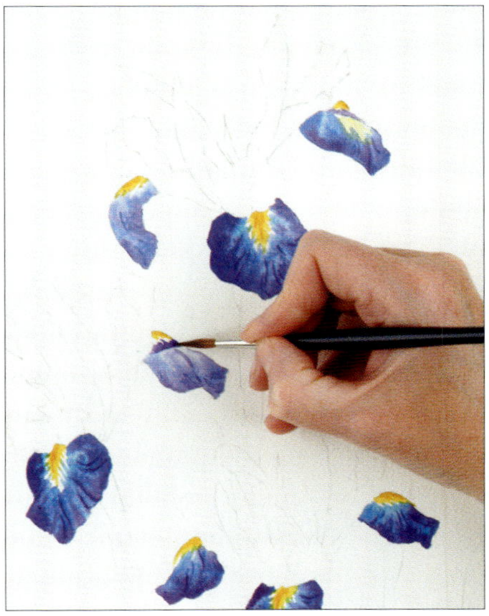

8 Using the deeper blue-purple mix, add the turnover on the top of the paler left-hand flower's petal. Leave to dry.

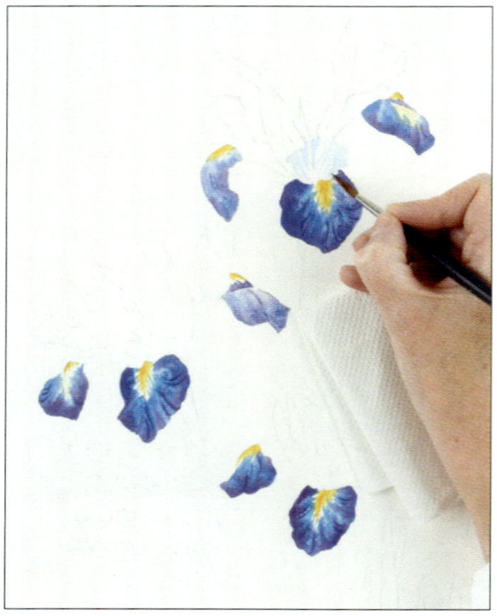

9 Prepare a pool of dilute French ultramarine and a pool of blue-purple: French ultramarine with a touch of permanent rose. Paint all the forward-facing, frilly-edged petals first, with the dilute French ultramarine, working inwards from the serrated edge, leaving white gaps to suggest folds.

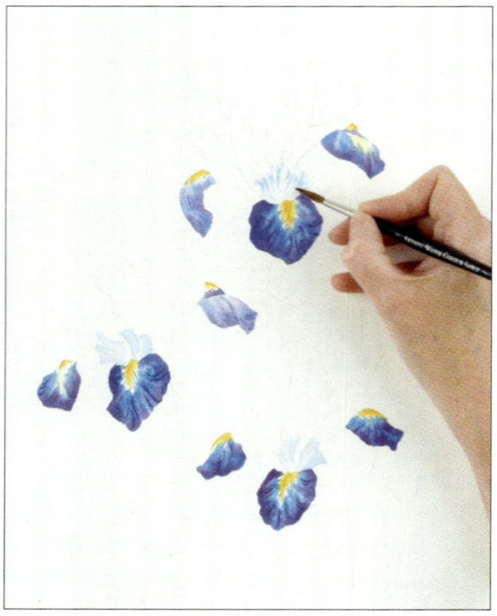

10 When the petals are dry, apply short, sweeping brushstrokes of the blue-purple mix over the paler blue frilly-edged petals to give greater depth and movement.

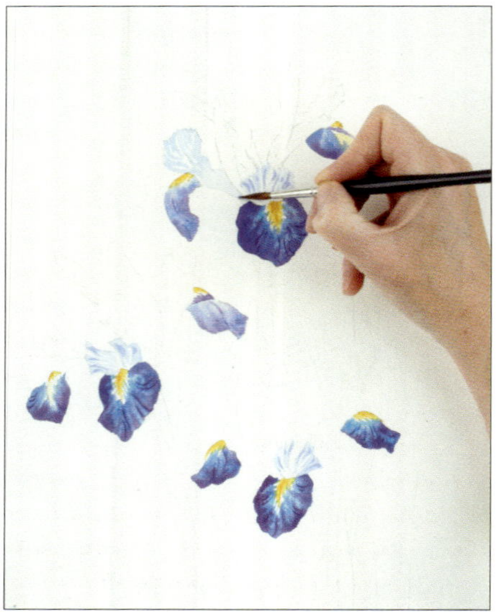

11 For the remaining frilly-edged petals, apply the dilute French ultramarine on dry paper as before, varying the tones by softening with a damp brush. Work inwards, adding water to create a paler wash towards the centre of the flower.

Tip

When painting the recessed folds of the petal, apply more pressure for a broader brushstroke on the outer edge and gradually taper the brush inwards to a fine point.

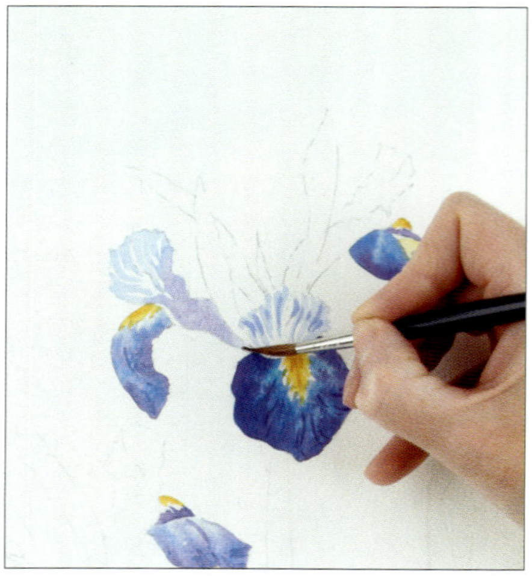

12 While this is damp, drop a pink-purple mix: permanent rose with a little French ultramarine into the base wash. Paint all of the larger, frilly-edged petals in this way, working from the top to the bottom, and from left to right.

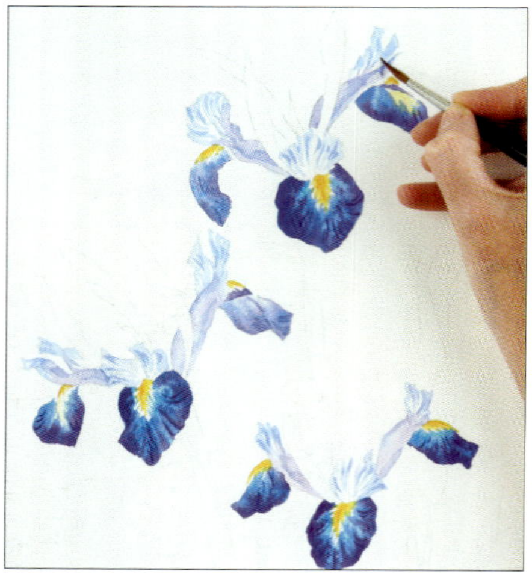

13 To define the shapes of the petals, prepare two stronger washes: a blue-purple and a pink-purple. Working wet-on-dry, apply sweeping brushstrokes using the blue-purple on the frilled edges and the pink-purple on the main curved area, diffusing here and there with water to add form.

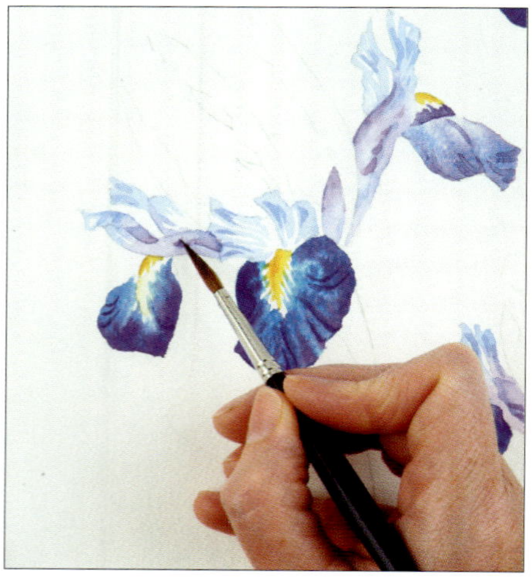

14 To add further depth, apply a stronger mix of pink-purple in a few areas, softening the edges with water.

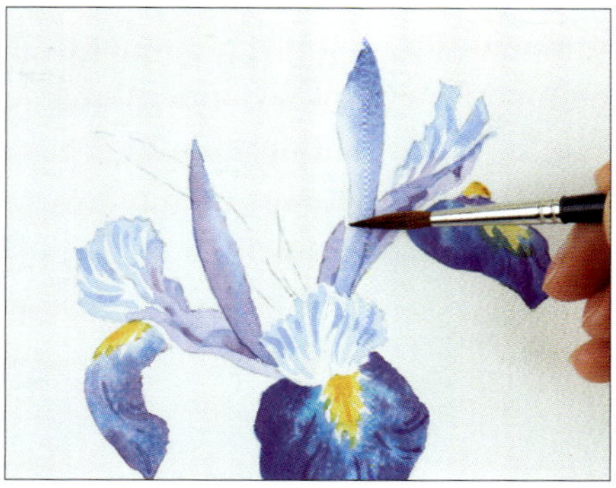

15 For the finer, top petals, make a blue-purple pool of French ultramarine with a tiny amount of permanent rose, a pool of cerulean blue and a pink-purple mix of permanent rose with a touch of French ultramarine. Using the blue-purple mix, run the brush along the curved edge, wet-on-dry. Work your brushstrokes in the direction of the growth of the petal, adding a little water to soften and diffuse the paint. While this is wet, drop in cerulean blue to vary the colours.

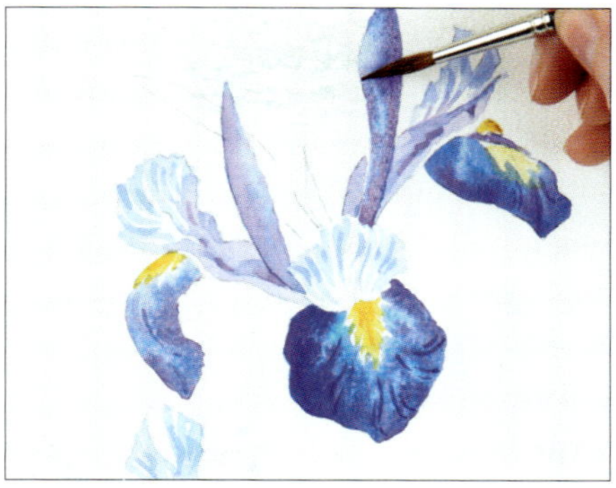

16 While this is still damp, using the pink-purple mix, run the brush over the base shade with a sweeping movement in the direction of the petal growth to create a variegated wash. Work from the base of the petal upwards. Where the petals overlap, leave one to dry before applying the wash to the adjacent petal. Paint all the petals in the same way, varying the colours, and allowing them to mix on the paper wet-in-wet. Allow to dry.

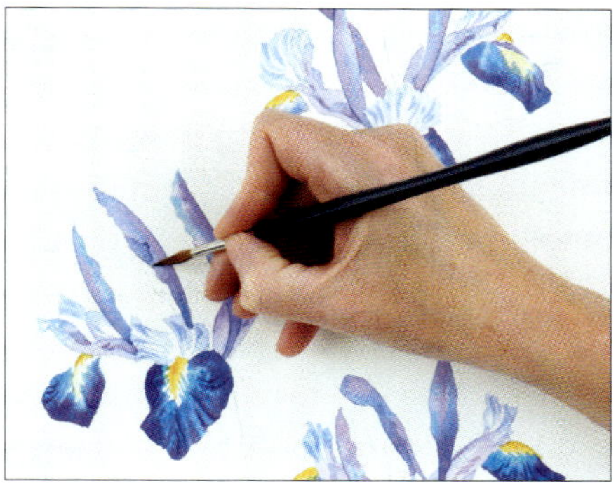

17 Where the inside of the petal is seen, add more depth of colour to this area, wet-on-dry using a stronger mix of the blue-purple. Diffuse the colour slightly with a touch of water.

Tip

Any splashes of paint on the paper can be removed by dabbing the area with a clean brush dipped in a little water.

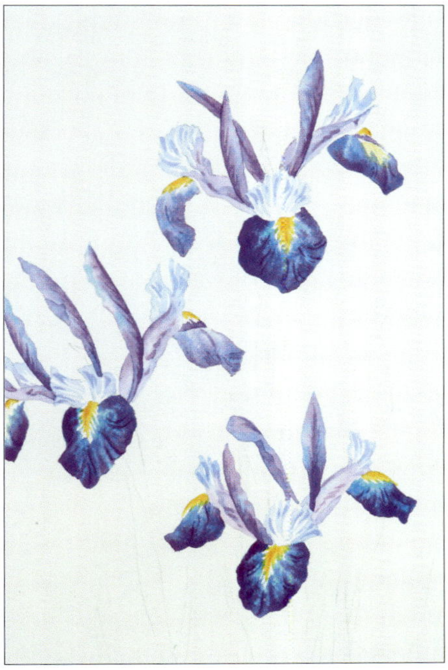

18 Using a stronger mix made of equal parts of French ultramarine and permanent rose, deepen the curved edge of these petals, sweeping the brush upwards from the base of the petal and towards the outer edge. The feathered-looking brushstrokes taper to a fine point to suggest the veins. Soften some with water.

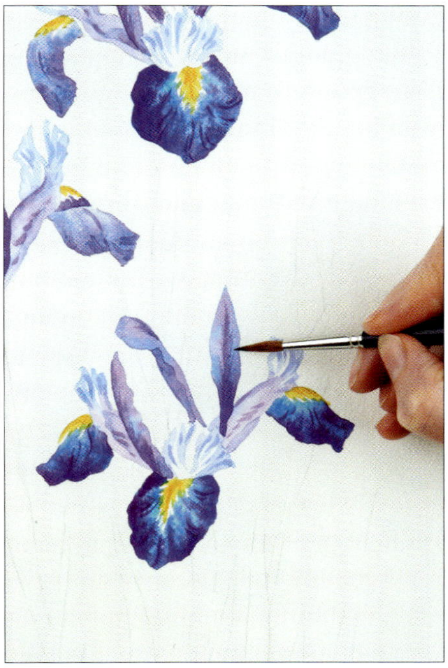

19 On the lower bloom, work on the petal which is face-on. Add more depth of colour lower down and draw the brush upwards along the central vein, pulling the brushstrokes to either side of it.

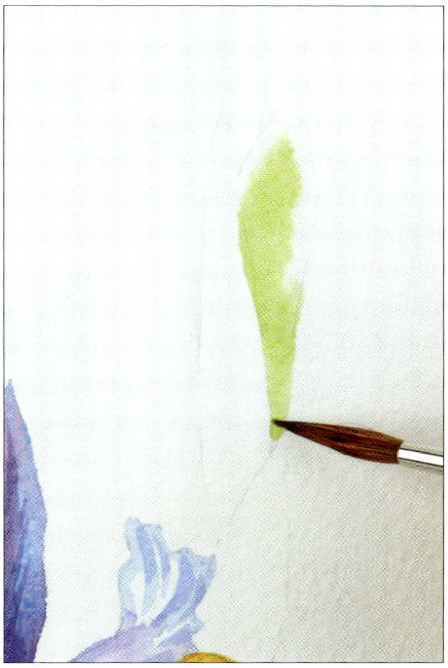

20 Prepare three pools of colour: a yellow-green: aureolin with a very small amount of French ultramarine, cerulean blue and a strong purple mix using equal parts of French ultramarine and permanent rose. Wet the bud area lightly and apply a light wash of the yellow-green.

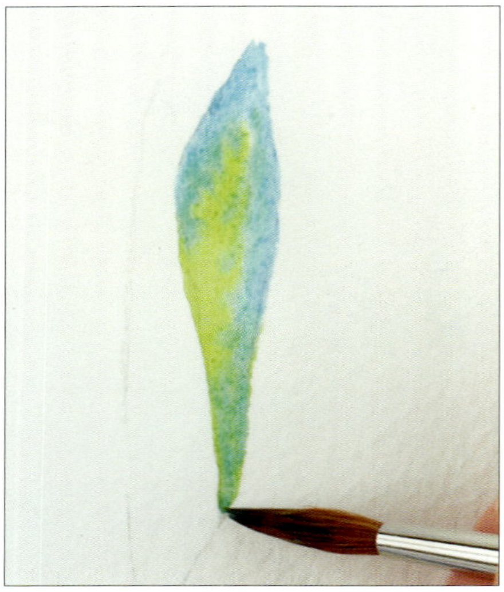

21 While this is wet, use the point of the brush to drop in cerulean blue around the edges to create a variegated wash.

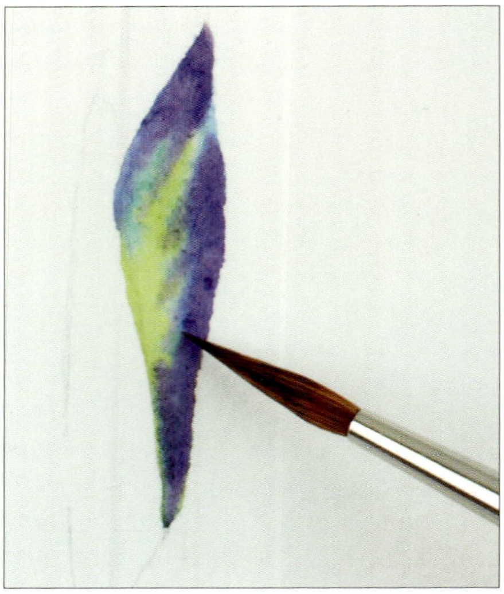

22 Continue working wet-in-wet and add in the purple mix. Drop in the colour at the tip of the bud and along the side, drawing a few brushstrokes over the green area.

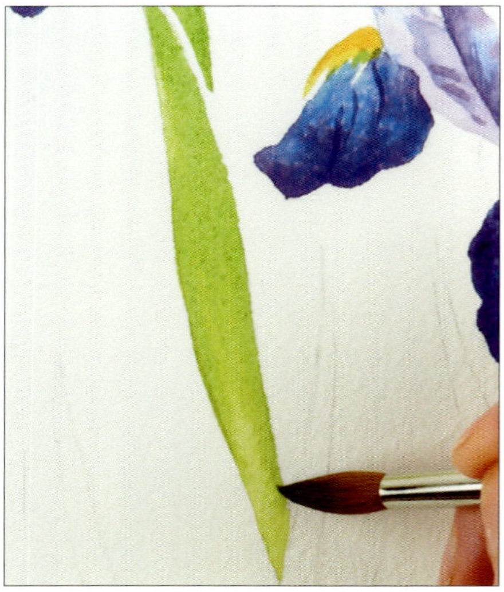

23 Prepare three shades of green using different proportions of the same two colours; a light yellow-green: aureolin with a tiny amount of French ultramarine, a mid-tone green using equal parts of aureolin and French ultramarine and a blue-green made up of French ultramarine with a small amount of aureolin. Using a size 8 round brush, apply a base wash wet-on-dry of the light yellow-green to each section of the leaves and stems, leaving a little gap of white paper between each section. While still damp, apply the mid-tone green and allow to dry slightly.

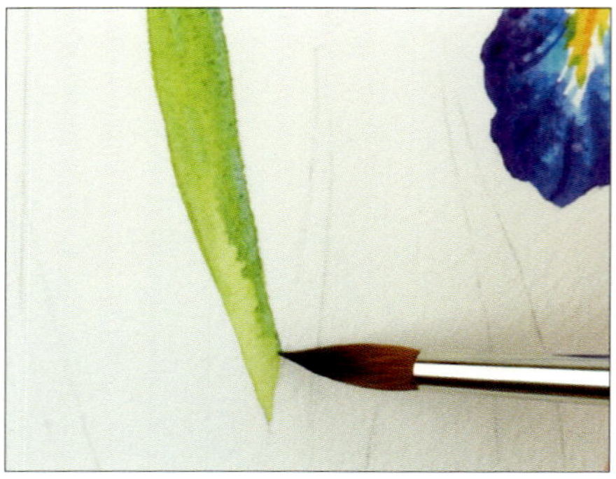

24 While slightly damp, add deeper tones of the cooler, but stronger blue-green mix to the stems and leaves to indicate areas of light and shade.

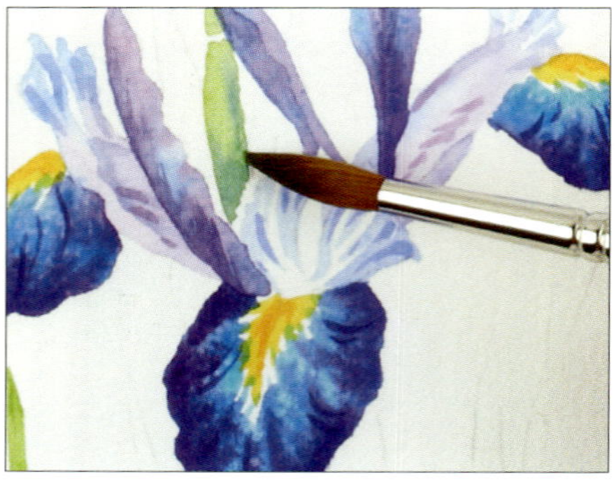

25 Continue using the cool blue-green mix, varying the tones where one leaf overlaps another. Apply the paint with sweeping brushstrokes, from either the top of the stems and leaves downwards or from the base upwards. Leave to dry.

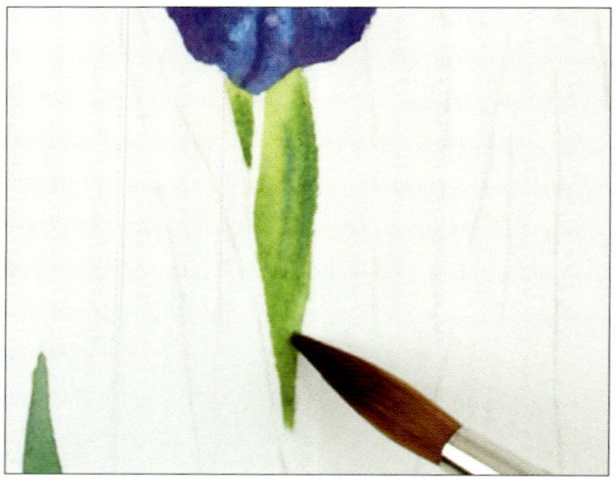

26 Prepare a stronger and warmer green made from equal parts of French ultramarine and new gamboge to balance the overall tones. Working wet-on-dry, and from the base of the leaves and stems upwards, add some further depth to the stems where required. Use a quick sweeping motion to suggest the veins. Add a touch of water here and there to diffuse the colour. Leave to dry. Remove any visible pencil lines with a clean eraser.

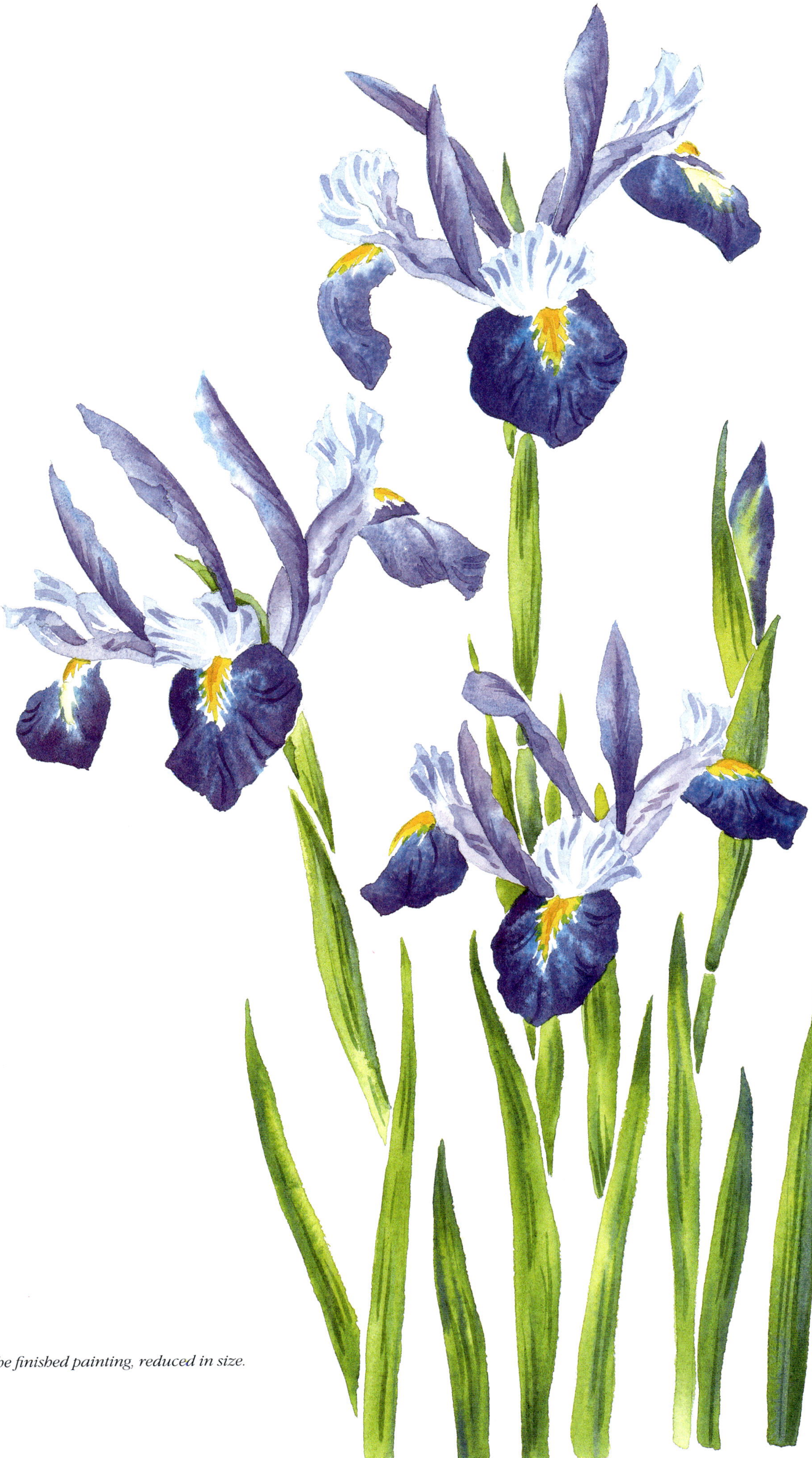

The finished painting, reduced in size.

Irises and Forget-me-nots

These delicate low-growing irises caught my eye, shooting up from the ground in early spring. Surrounded by forget-me-not flowers, they complemented each other perfectly. Looking closely at the iris petals, the varied mix of different shades of blue and mauve could be seen, which suggested a soft variegated wet-on-wet base of colours.

You will need

TRACING **2**

300gsm (140lb) Not watercolour paper

Colours: aureolin, new gamboge, cerulean blue, Winsor blue (green shade), cobalt blue, French ultramarine, quinacridone magenta, burnt sienna

Brushes: size 4 round, size 5 round, size 8 round

Pencils: 2B, H

Kitchen paper

Eraser

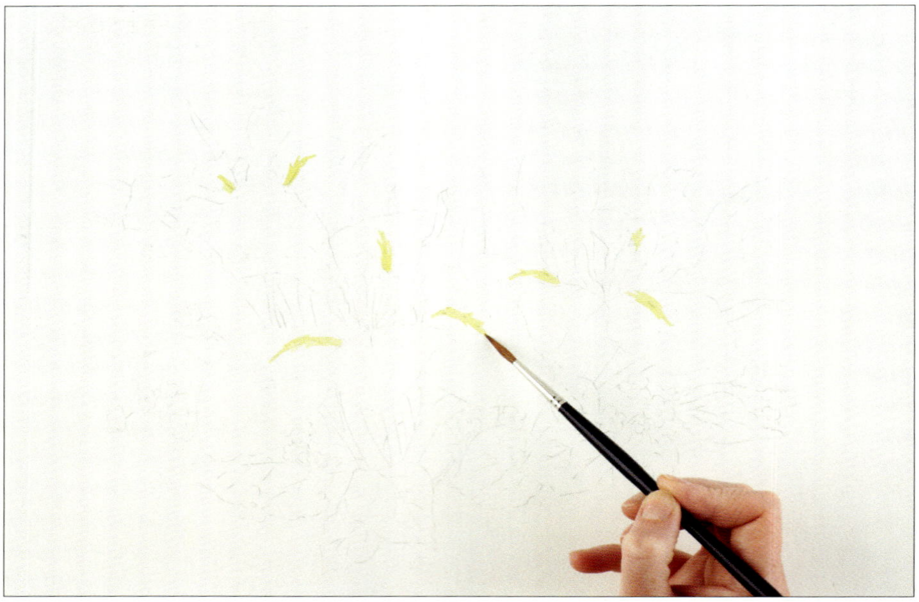

1 Transfer the image to the paper following the directions on page 9 and make a strong pool of aureolin. Using a size 5 round brush, paint in the yellow markings in the centre of each of the lower petals of each flower head, wet-on-dry. Work from the inside of the petal outwards with a broad stroke and feather a few brushstrokes either side of the central line. Leave to dry.

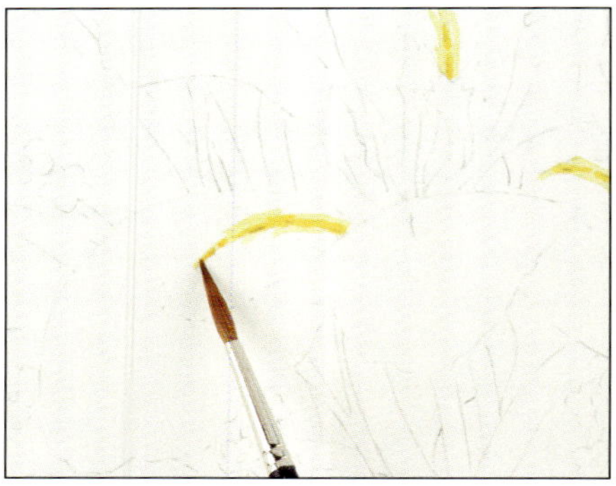

2 Make a strong pool of new gamboge and apply a broken brushstroke along the centre of the aureolin yellow base to add depth.

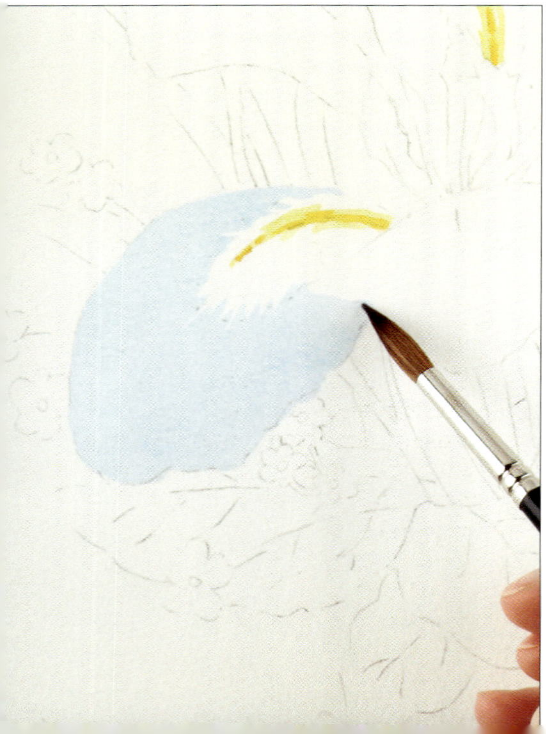

3 Make four further pools of colour: cobalt blue, French ultramarine, cerulean blue and a mix of quinacridone magenta and French ultramarine to make a pink-purple. Change to a size 8 round brush and glaze each of the petals with dilute cobalt blue. Work from the outside of the petal inwards, tapering the brush to give a feathered edge of white paper around the yellow stripe.

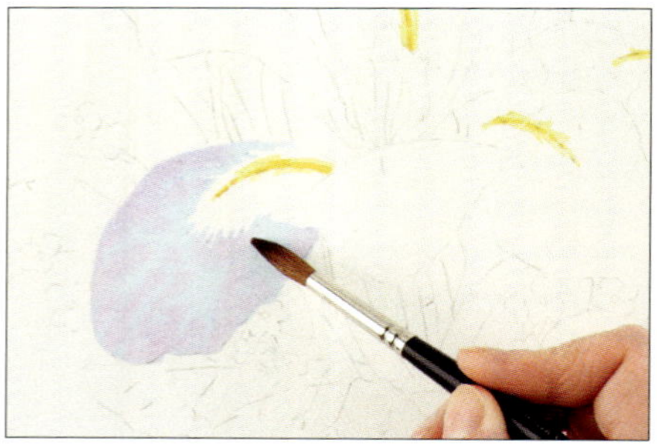

4 Whilst still wet, load your brush with the pink-purple mix and drop in some colour from the outer edge of the petal inwards. Let it blend naturally with the cobalt blue.

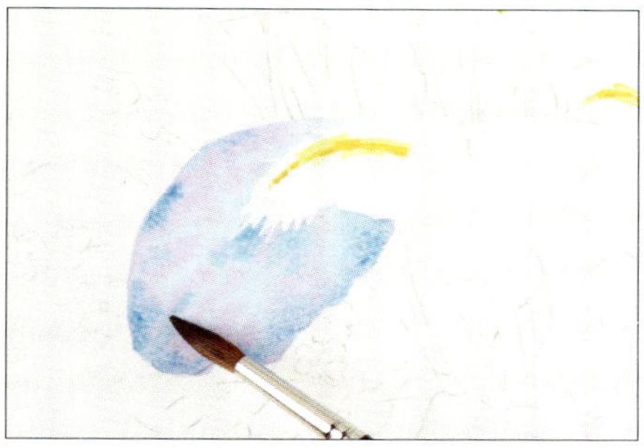

5 Add more depth and shape by dropping in cerulean blue, allowing the colours to blend.

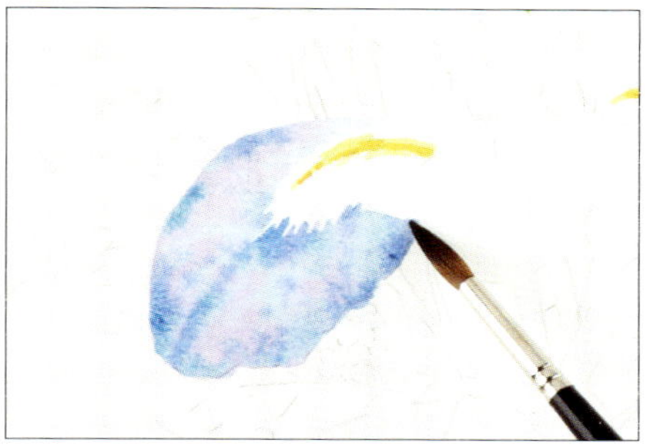

6 Shade the petal by dropping in French ultramarine, which granulates with the cerulean blue to create a softly textured, variegated base. Pull a few brushstrokes towards the outer edge of the petal to suggest recesses and veins.

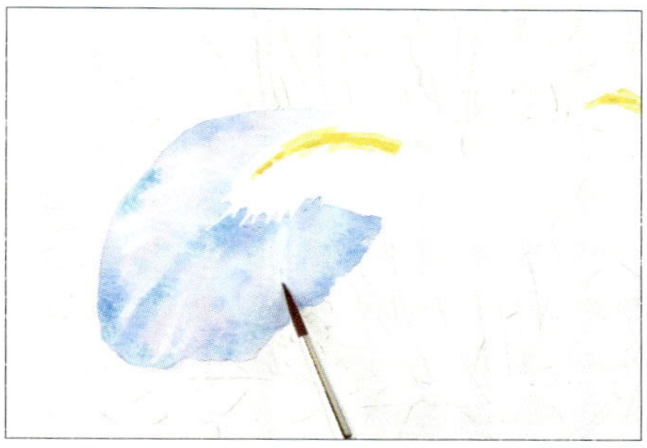

7 Take a size 4 round brush and rinse it in clean water. Dab it on to a piece of kitchen paper to take out the excess water and use to take out a few highlights on the petal.

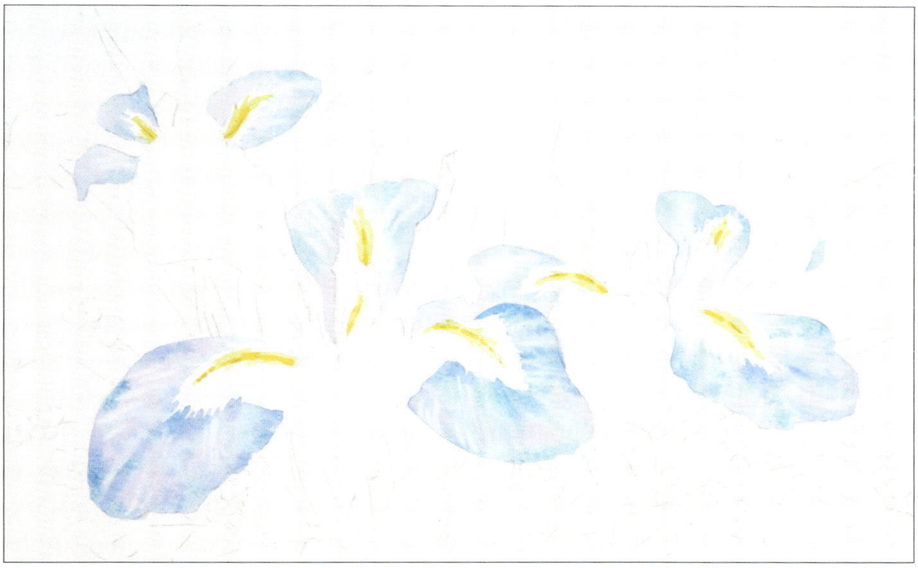

8 Repeat steps 3–7 for the rest of the yellow-centred petals.

Tip

When you lift out highlights, dab your brush on to kitchen paper to remove the lifted-out paint before rinsing again and continuing.

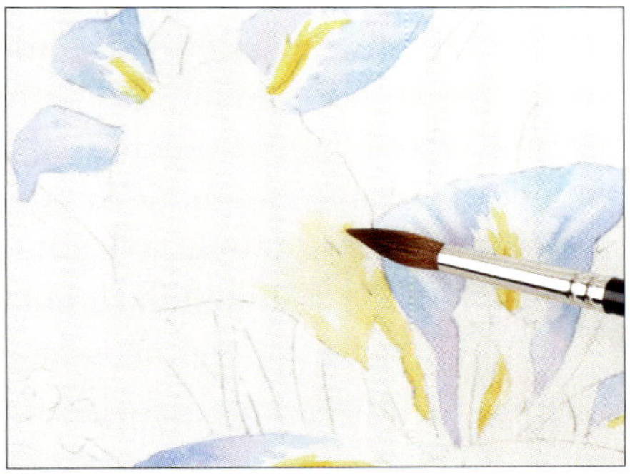

9 Using a size 8 round brush, glaze one of the remaining alternate petals with water. Apply new gamboge to the base of the petal and gently ease the colour upwards.

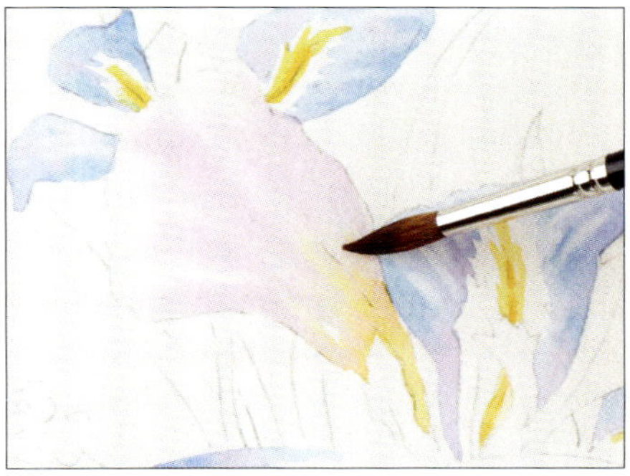

10 Using the pink-purple mix, apply sweeping brushstrokes from the tip of the petal downwards towards the yellow base so that the two colours merge. Leave some white gaps of paper for highlights.

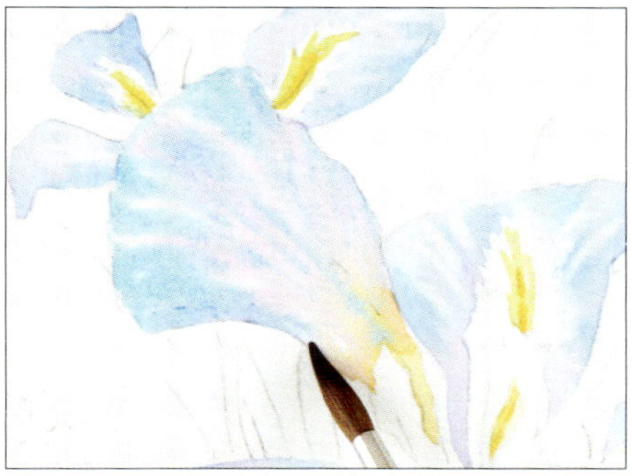

11 Load your brush with cerulean blue and, while still damp, draw brushstrokes from the outer edge inwards. Leave white gaps for highlights and let the colours blend together.

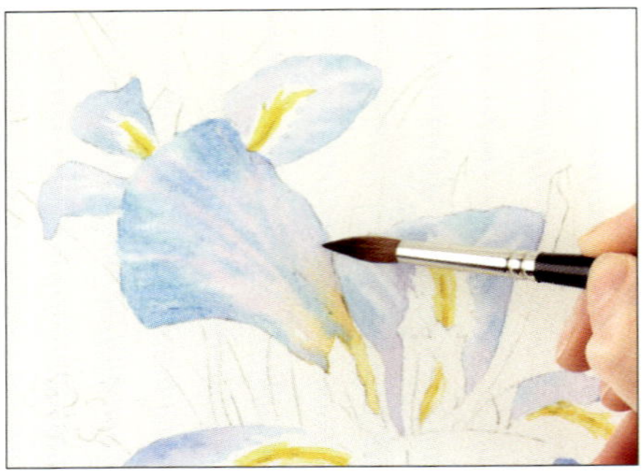

12 Drop in some French ultramarine along the edges and towards the centre to suggest the form of the petal.

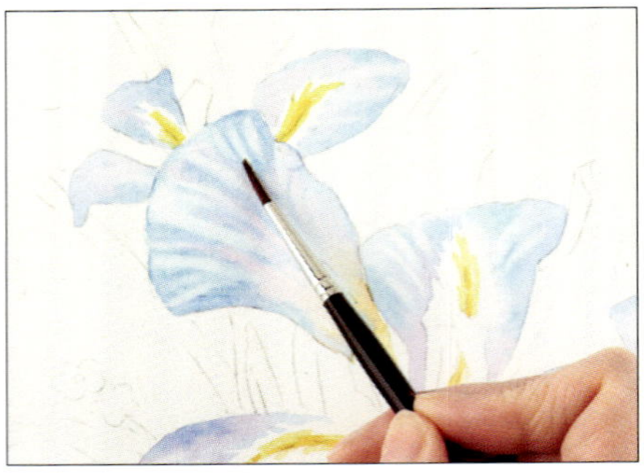

13 Change to a size 4 round brush and lift out some highlights using the same technique as described in step 7.

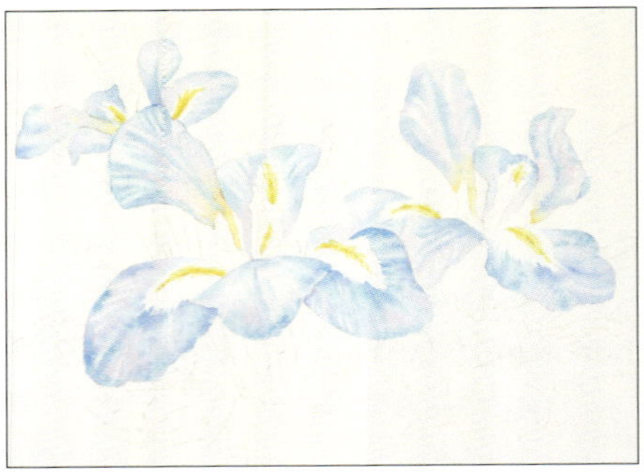

14 Repeat steps 9–13 for the rest of the petals except for the curled one in the centre.

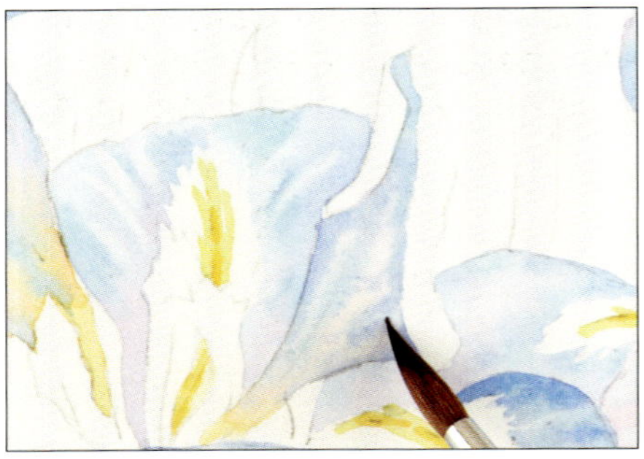

15 Using a size 8 brush, glaze the curled petal in the centre with water, leaving the curled areas dry. Apply the same sequences of variegated wash as in steps 9–13. Leave to dry.

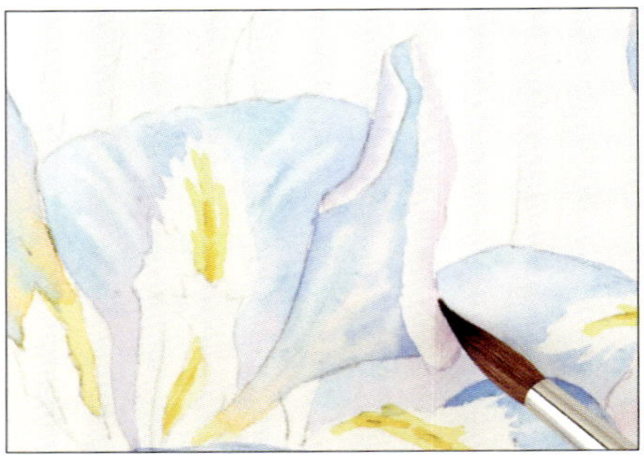

16 Carefully glaze the curled areas of this petal with water. Load your brush with the pink-purple mix and run the brush along the outer edge of the curled area so that the colour flows inwards.

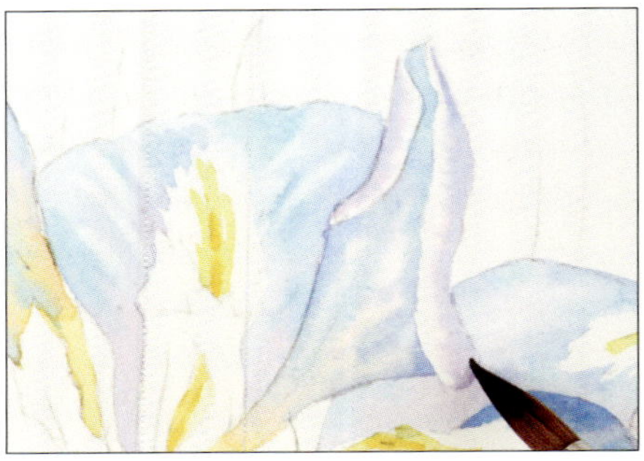

17 While still wet, run your brush, loaded with French ultramarine, down from the tip to the base of this curled area and allow the colours to blend into each other.

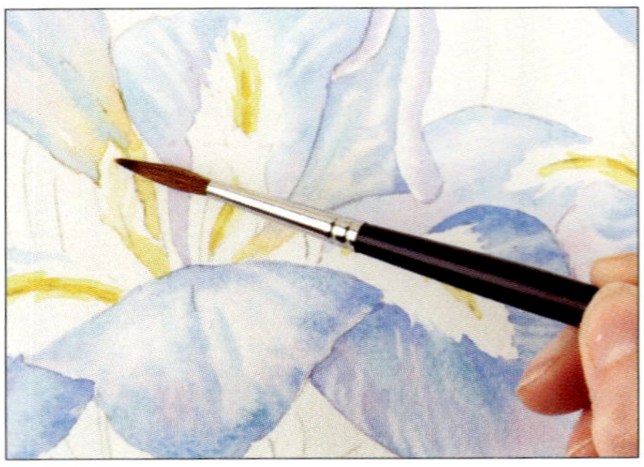

18 Change to a size 5 round brush and, apply a very dilute wash of new gamboge wet-on-dry to the small, central, serrated petals. Leave areas white to suggest veins and soften, leaving an edge of white.

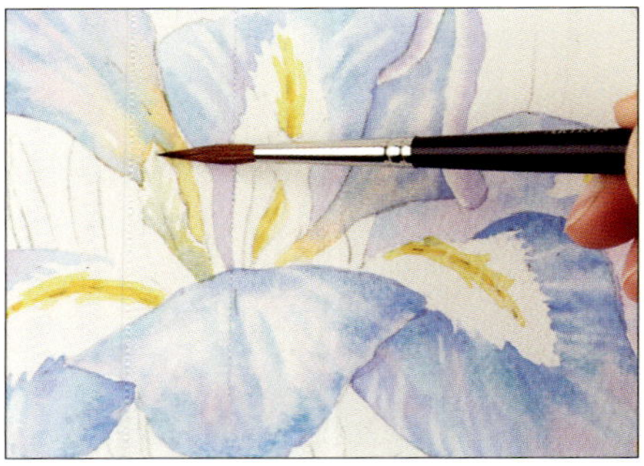

19 Prepare a pool of equal parts of French ultramarine and burnt sienna to make a grey mix. Working wet-in-wet, draw your brush along the central vein, allowing it to merge with the yellow base. Leave to dry.

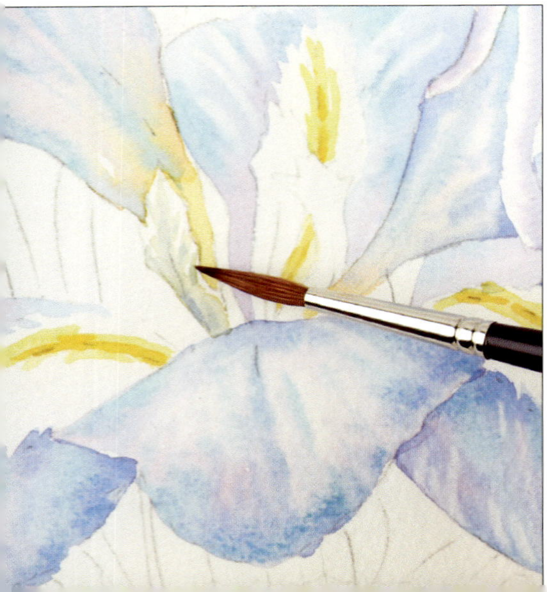

20 Using the grey mix, wet-on-dry, draw your brush down the central line and soften it to suggest depth in this area.

Tip

Rather than use pure grey to suggest shadow, apply a base of yellow first. This will lift and give more life to the grey.

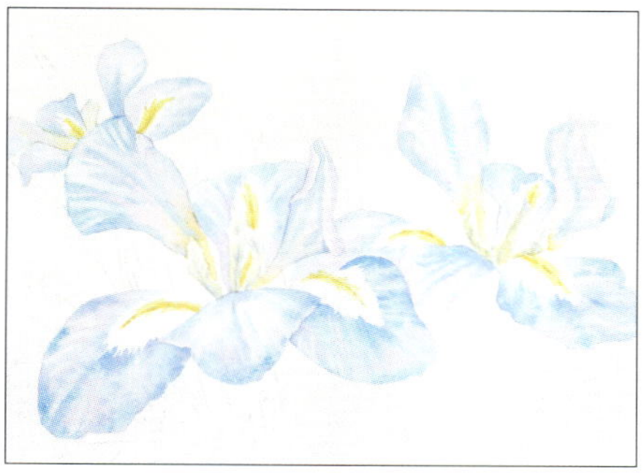

21 Repeat steps 18–20 for all the other inner petals.

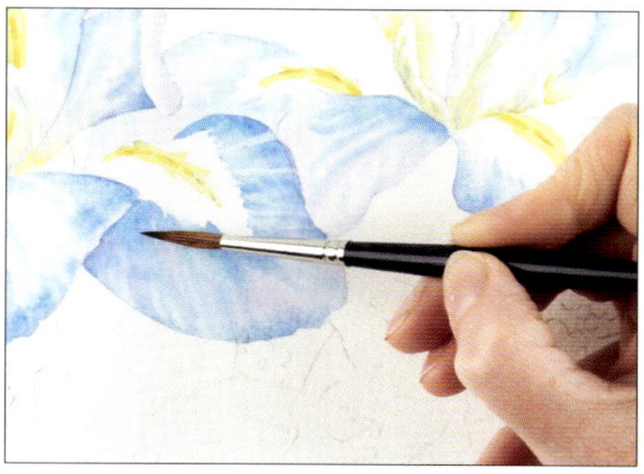

22 Where the petals overlap or strong shadows fall on the edges of the petals, in recesses and on fluted edges, apply a little French ultramarine to give a shadowed effect. Blend in with the base colours by softening the edges with a little water. Leave to dry.

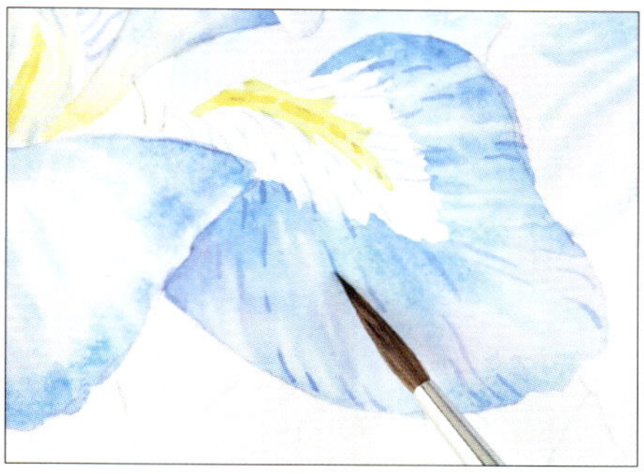

23 Vein the petals with a mix of French ultramarine with a tiny touch of quinacridone magenta, drawing the tip of the size 5 round from the centre outwards, following the contour of the petal. Continue on each petal, adding a few sweeping brushstrokes from the outer edge in.

Tip

You don't need to paint in *every* vein and marking on the petals and leaves. Just suggesting these details will be sufficient to convey the form of the plant and the direction of growth.

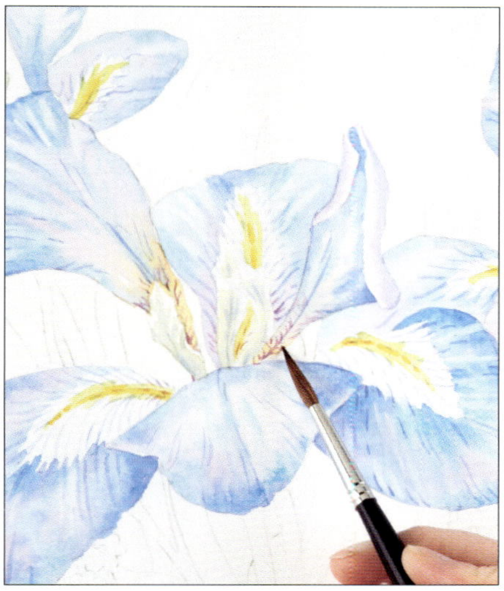

24 Add the deeper red veins using the tip of your brush, with a mix of quinacridone magenta with a touch of French ultramarine.

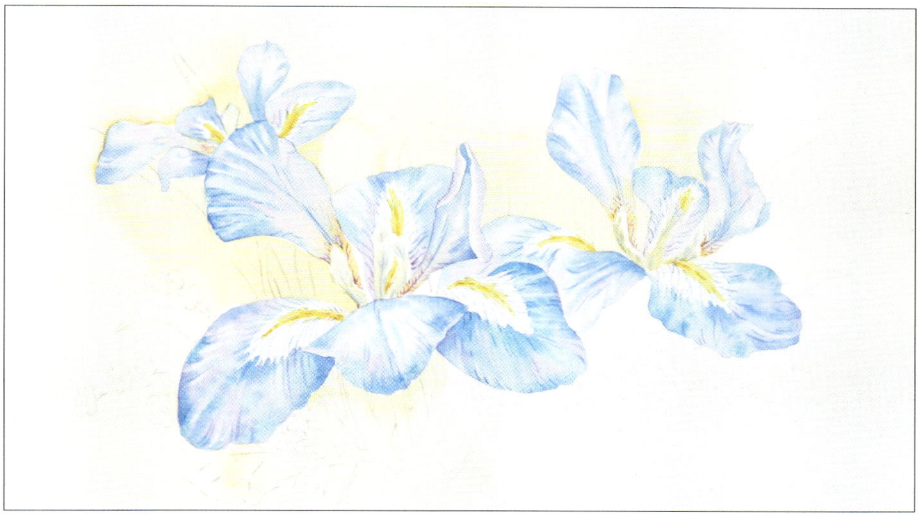

25 Prepare a dilute pool of new gamboge mixed with a very small amount of quinacridone magenta to make a warm yellow. With a loaded size 8 brush, apply a wash around each flower head and diffuse with water towards the edges. The colour should be at its strongest around the central flowers. Apply the wash over the pencil lines of the small flowers and leaves.

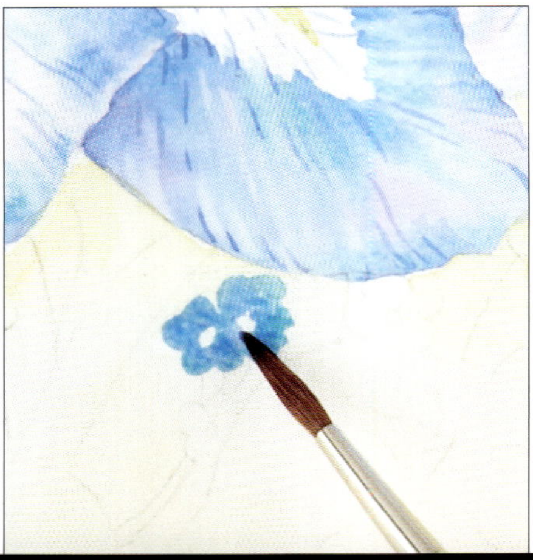

26 Prepare two pools: cerulean blue and French ultramarine. Using a size 5 round brush, paint in the forget-me-nots in cerulean, leaving a white circle in the centre. Drop in a little French ultramarine around each centre. Leave to dry.

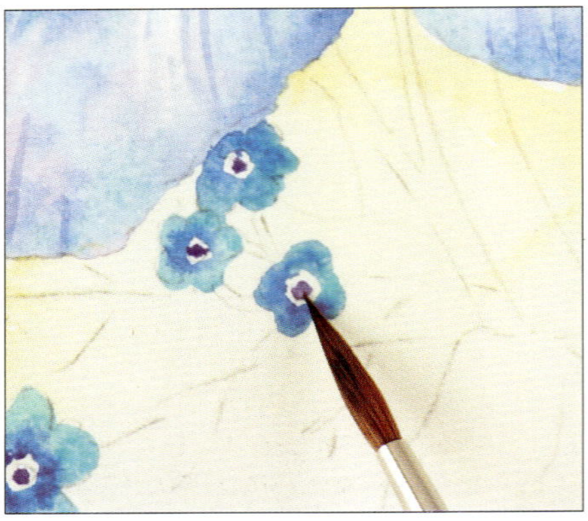

27 Prepare a mix of equal parts of quinacridone magenta and French ultramarine. Using the tip of your brush, dot the paint in the centre of each forget-me-not flower.

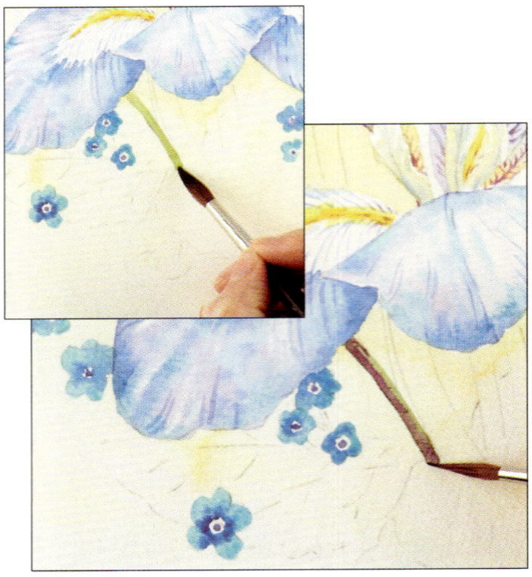

28 Prepare two pools of colour: equal parts of French ultramarine and new gamboge to make green, and quinacridone magenta mixed with French ultramarine to make a pink-purple. Paint the forget-me-not stems with a base wash of the green. While still wet, draw your brush down the left-hand shaded side of the stem in the pink-purple, allowing the colours to blend.

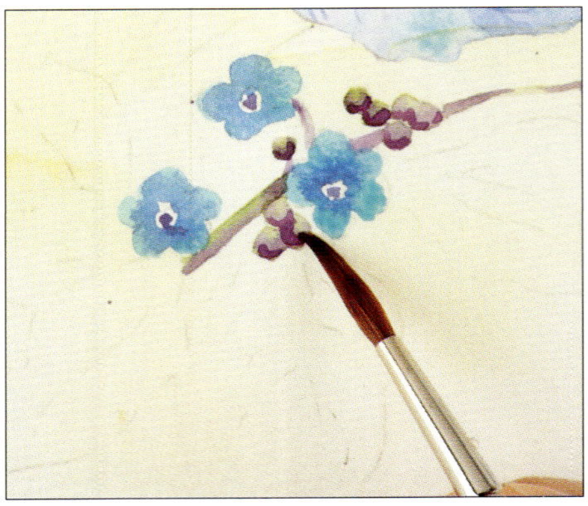

29 Paint in the forget-me-not buds using the same colours and method as the stems. When dry, use a stronger wash of the pink-purple mix to add depth and shadow to the buds.

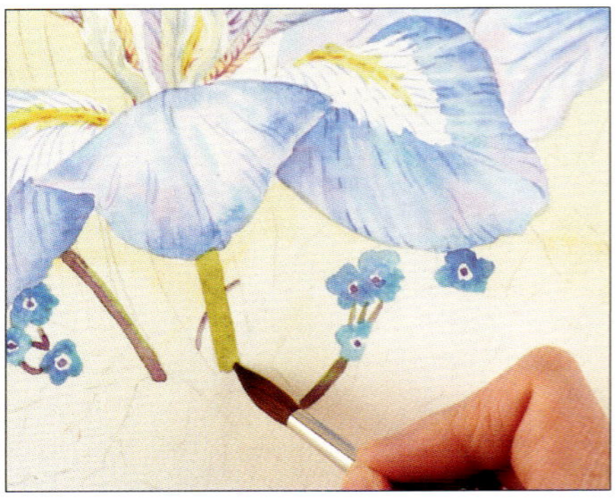

30 Prepare two pools: equal parts of new gamboge with French ultramarine for a yellow-green, and predominantly more French ultramarine with new gamboge for a blue-green. Using a size 8 round brush, apply the yellow-green wash on the iris stem in a sweeping motion from top to bottom.

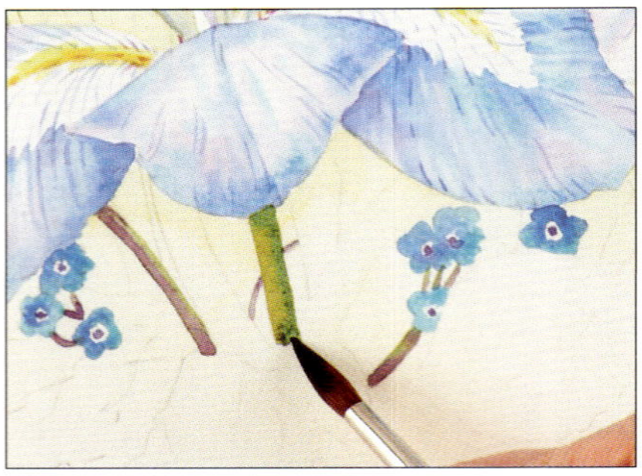

31 On the shaded side of the stem, sweep the blue-green colour from the top of the stem to the bottom while the base is still wet. Allow the colour to bleed across slightly to suggest the roundness of the stem.

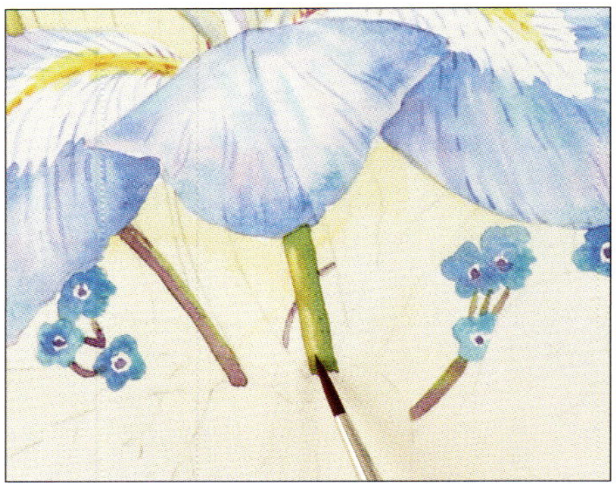

32 Taking a size 4 round brush, lift some highlights out of the lighter side of the stem, whilst slightly damp.

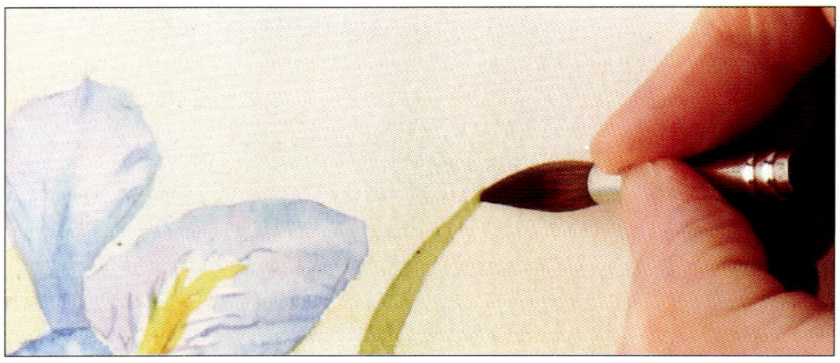

33 For the foreground spiky iris leaves, use a size 8 round brush and apply a base wash of the yellow-green mix, working from the base upwards to the tip.

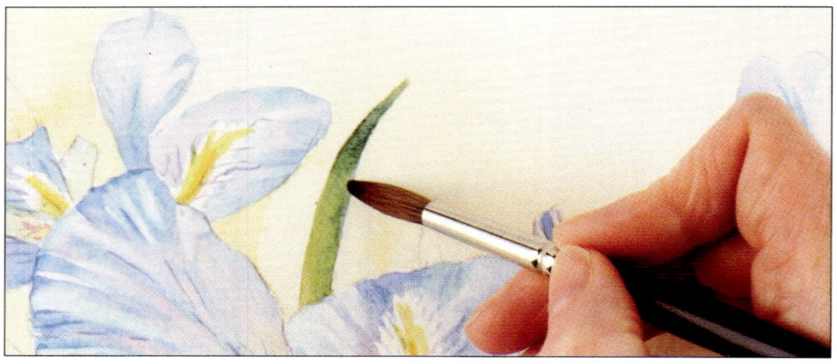

34 Whilst still wet, load your brush with the blue-green and drop it in where there are deeper shadowed tones. Allow the blue-green to blend into the base colour. Work on all the foreground leaves in this way.

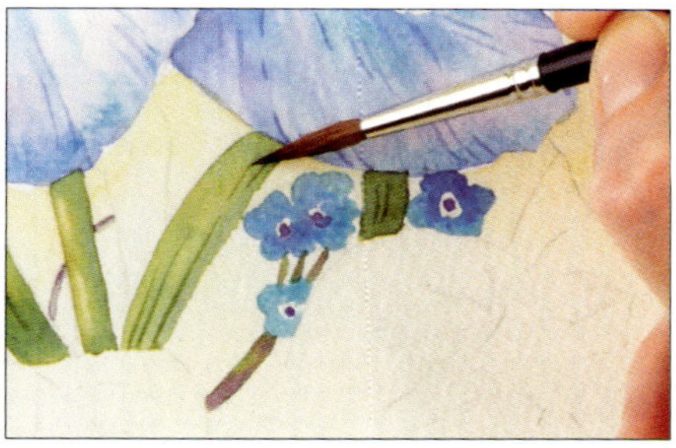

35 Return to a size 5 round brush and, using a stronger mix of French ultramarine and new gamboge, add suggestions of the fine veins, working the point of the brush from the base upwards.

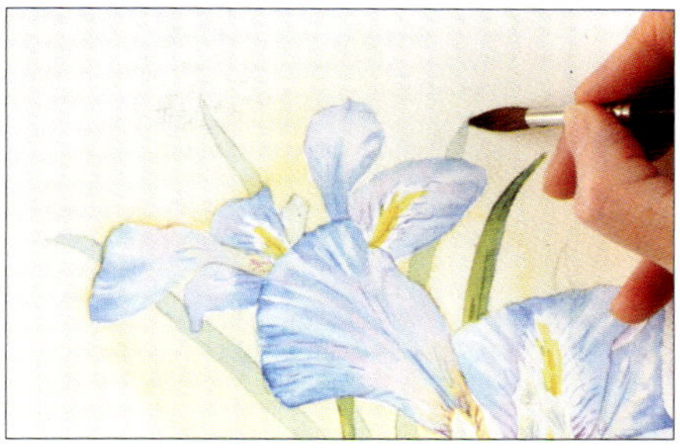

36 Change to a size 8 round brush. Dilute the blue-green mix and apply it to the pointed iris leaves in the background, working from the base to the tips.

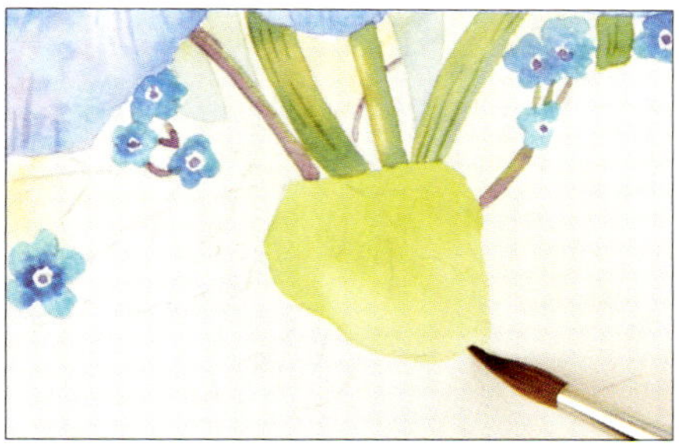

37 For the forget-me not leaves, apply the yellow-green mix wet-on-dry and diffuse with water towards the tip of the leaf to vary the tone.

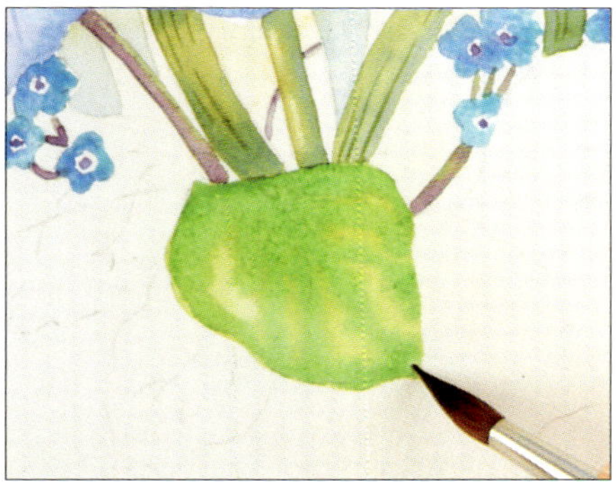

38 Prepare a fresh green using a mix of Winsor blue (green shade) and new gamboge. While damp, draw the brush down the centre of the leaf and out towards either side to suggest the veins. Leave to dry slightly.

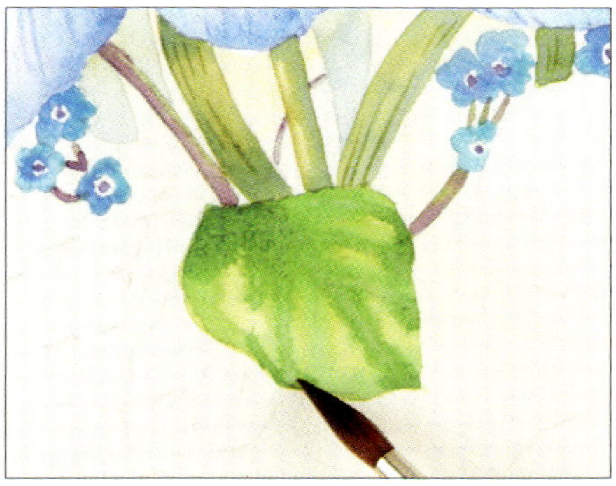

39 Prepare a stronger green mix of French ultramarine and aureolin. Again, using the point of the brush, pull the colour down towards the tip of the leaf and either side to add more depth and form. Leave to dry.

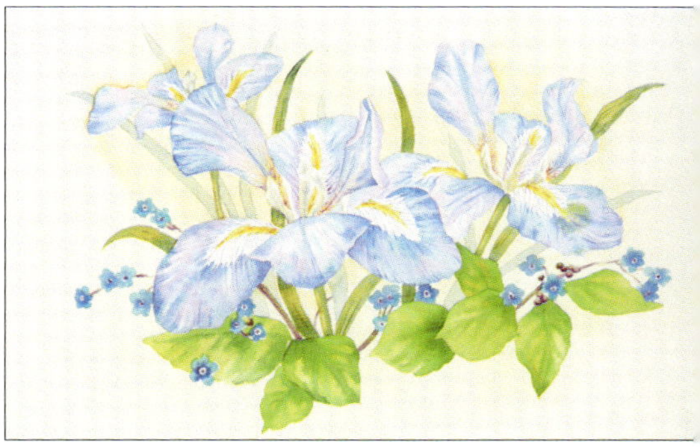

40 Build up the remaining forget-me-not leaves in this way, varying the shades so they are not too uniform. Where the leaves overlap, those underneath can be painted with more of the blue-green to suggest shadow.

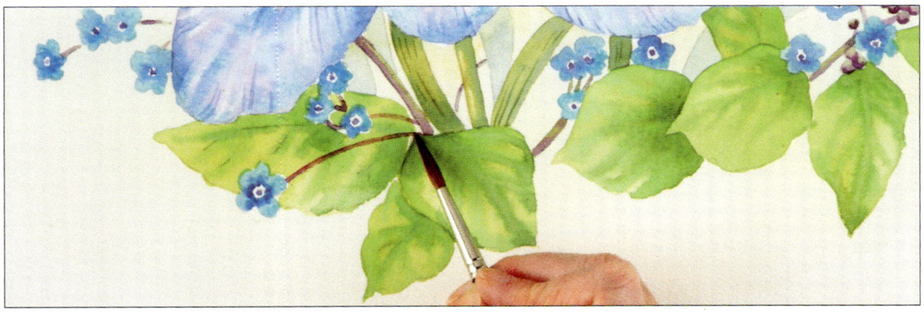

41 Using a mix of quinacridone magenta plus a dash of French ultramarine, paint in the forget-me-not stems which overlap the leaves with a size 5 round brush.

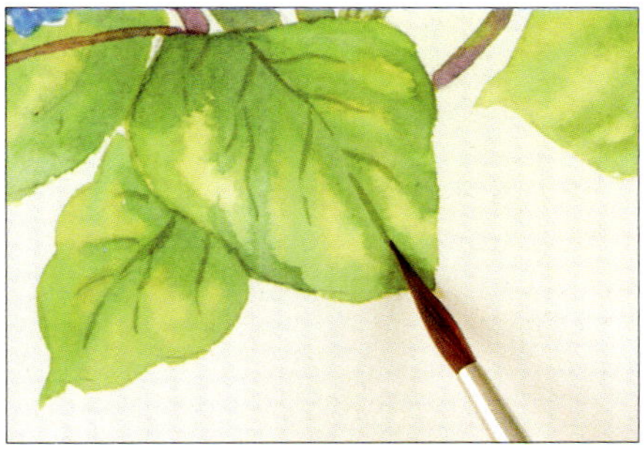

42 Prepare a stronger mix of equal parts of French ultramarine and new gamboge. Working from the base to the tip of each leaf, paint in the central vein and some fine secondary veins. Repeat for all of the forget-me-not leaves. Leave to dry and remove any visible pencil lines with a clean eraser.

Tip

Where the leaves overlap, be sure to paint the leaf underneath first and leave it to dry completely before working on the leaf on top.

Overleaf
The finished painting.

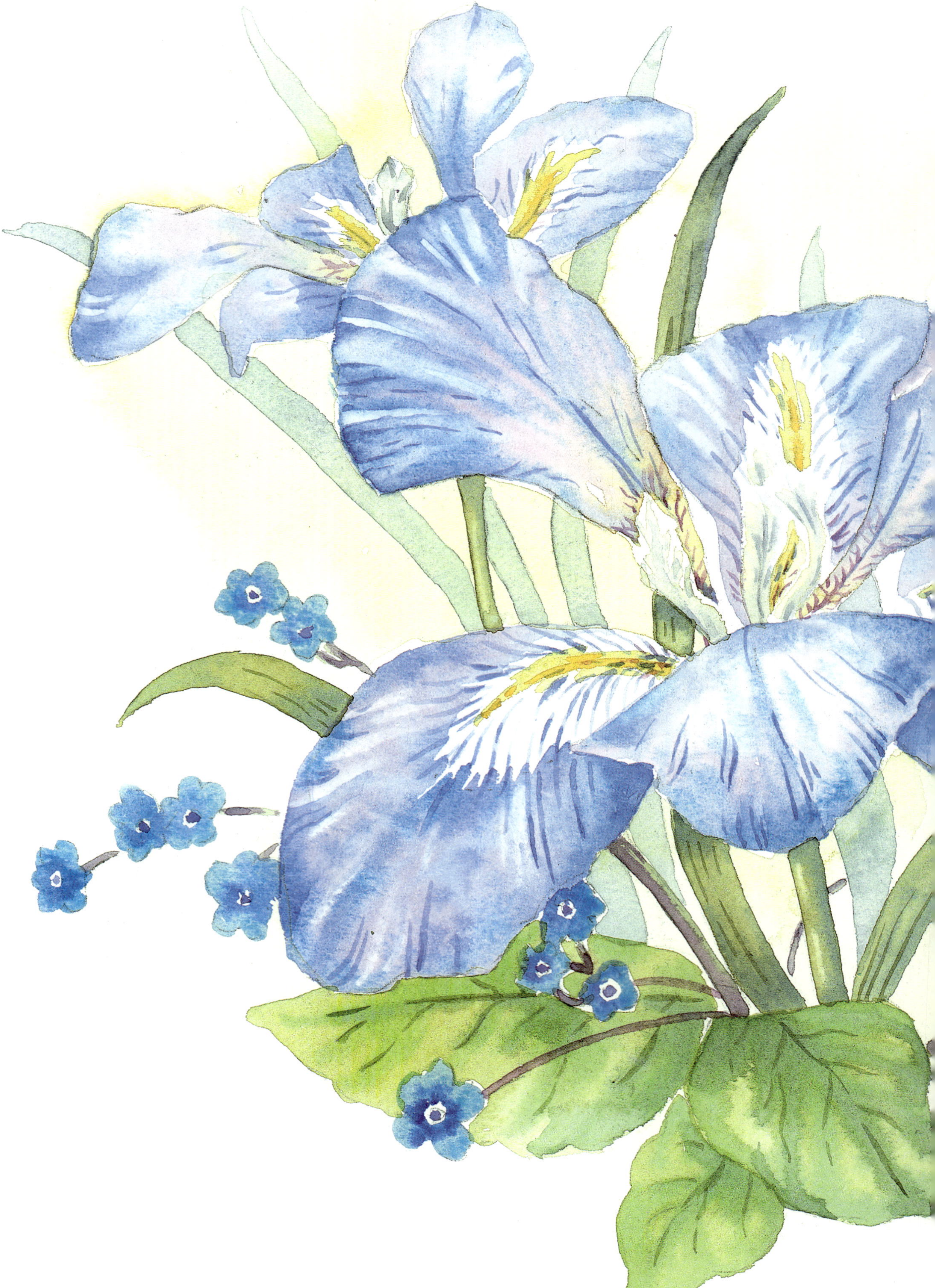

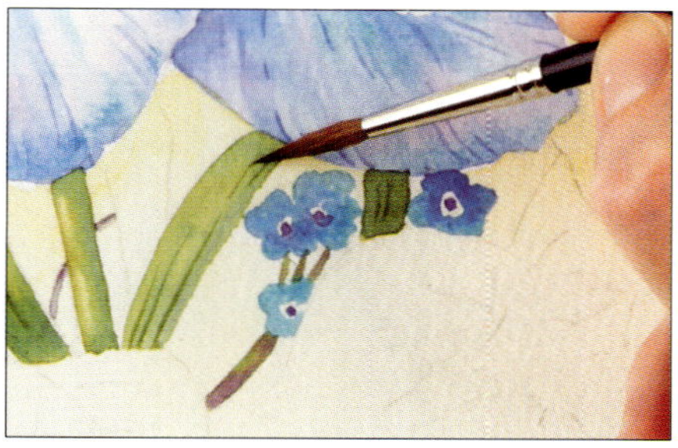

35 Return to a size 5 round brush and, using a stronger mix of French ultramarine and new gamboge, add suggestions of the fine veins, working the point of the brush from the base upwards.

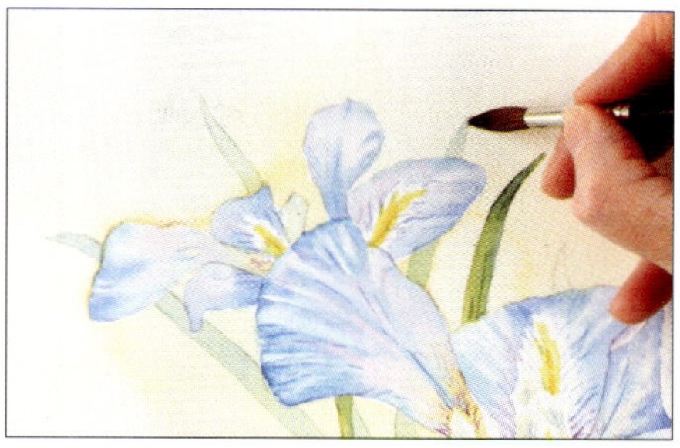

36 Change to a size 8 round brush. Dilute the blue-green mix and apply it to the pointed iris leaves in the background, working from the base to the tips.

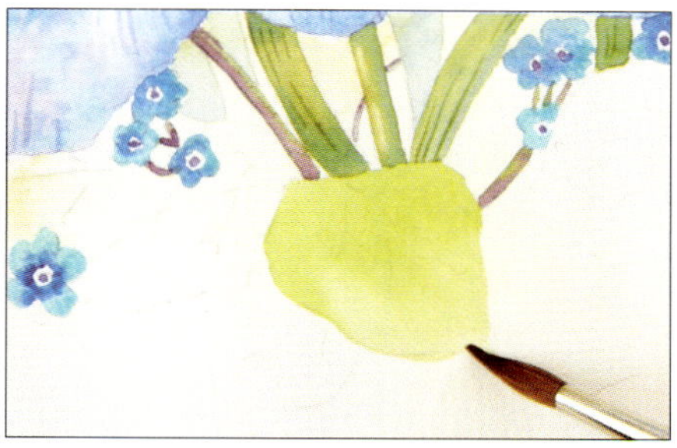

37 For the forget-me not leaves, apply the yellow-green mix wet-on-dry and diffuse with water towards the tip of the leaf to vary the tone.

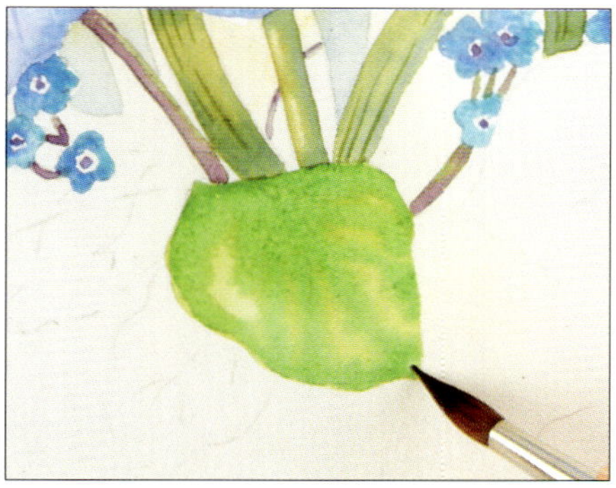

38 Prepare a fresh green using a mix of Winsor blue (green shade) and new gamboge. While damp, draw the brush down the centre of the leaf and out towards either side to suggest the veins. Leave to dry slightly.

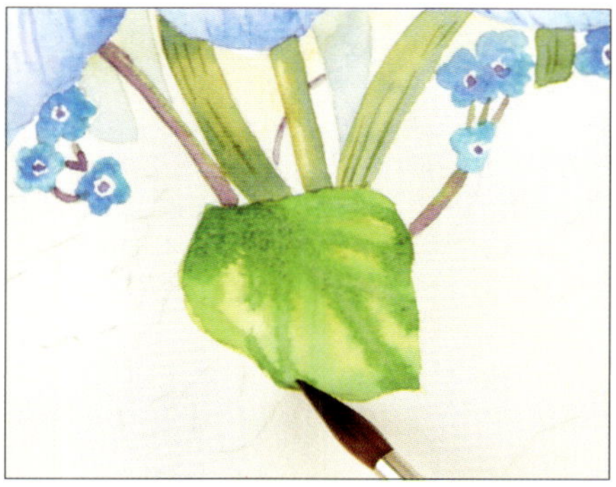

39 Prepare a stronger green mix of French ultramarine and aureolin. Again, using the point of the brush, pull the colour down towards the tip of the leaf and either side to add more depth and form. Leave to dry.

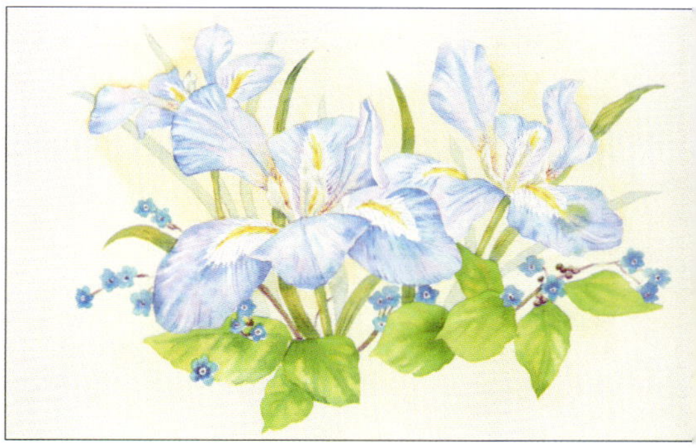

40 Build up the remaining forget-me-not leaves in this way, varying the shades so they are not too uniform. Where the leaves overlap, those underneath can be painted with more of the blue-green to suggest shadow.

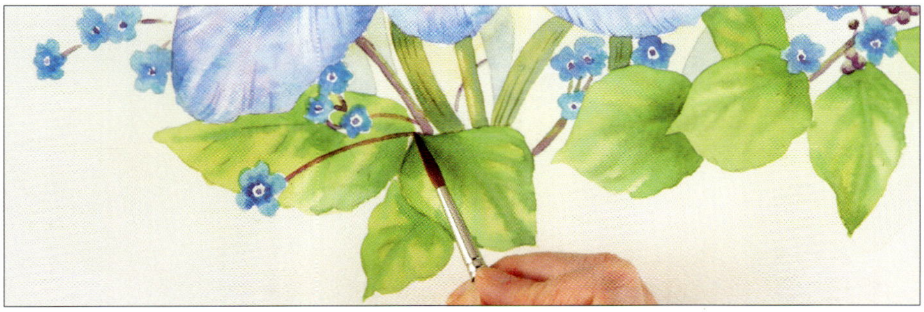

41 Using a mix of quinacridone magenta plus a dash of French ultramarine, paint in the forget-me-not stems which overlap the leaves with a size 5 round brush.

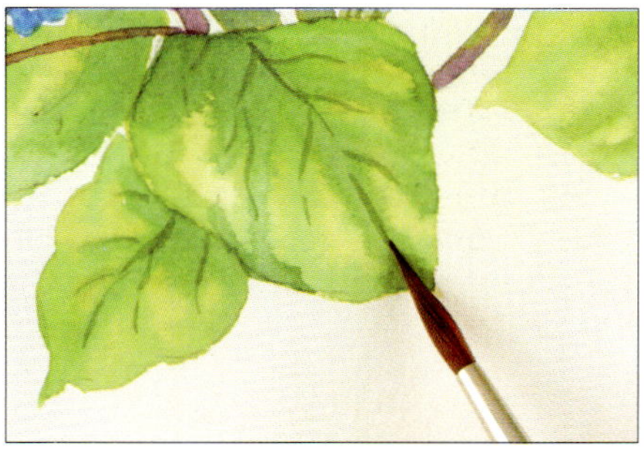

42 Prepare a stronger mix of equal parts of French ultramarine and new gamboge. Working from the base to the tip of each leaf, paint in the central vein and some fine secondary veins. Repeat for all of the forget-me-not leaves. Leave to dry and remove any visible pencil lines with a clean eraser.

Tip

Where the leaves overlap, be sure to paint the leaf underneath first and leave it to dry completely before working on the leaf on top.

Overleaf
The finished painting.

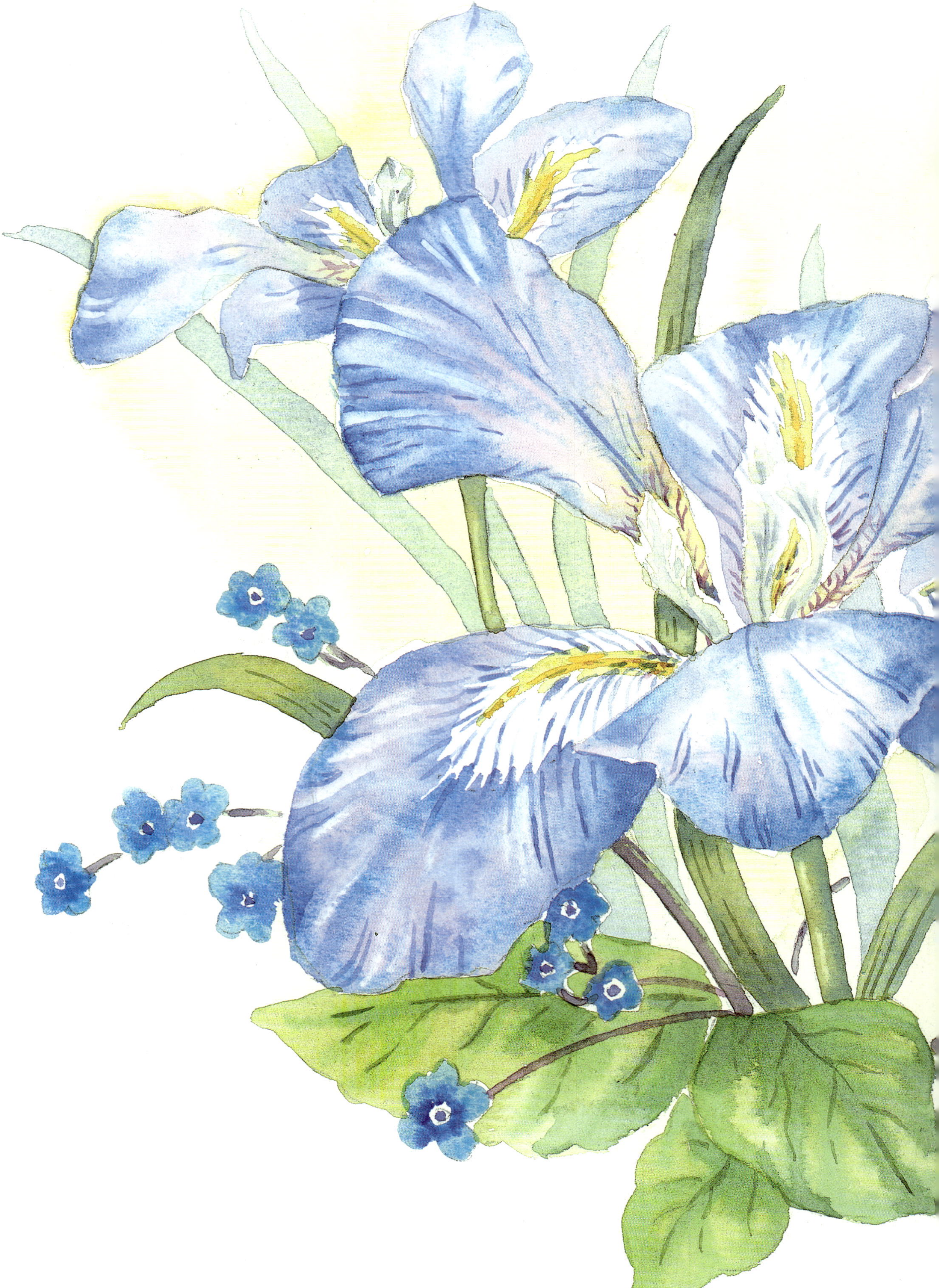

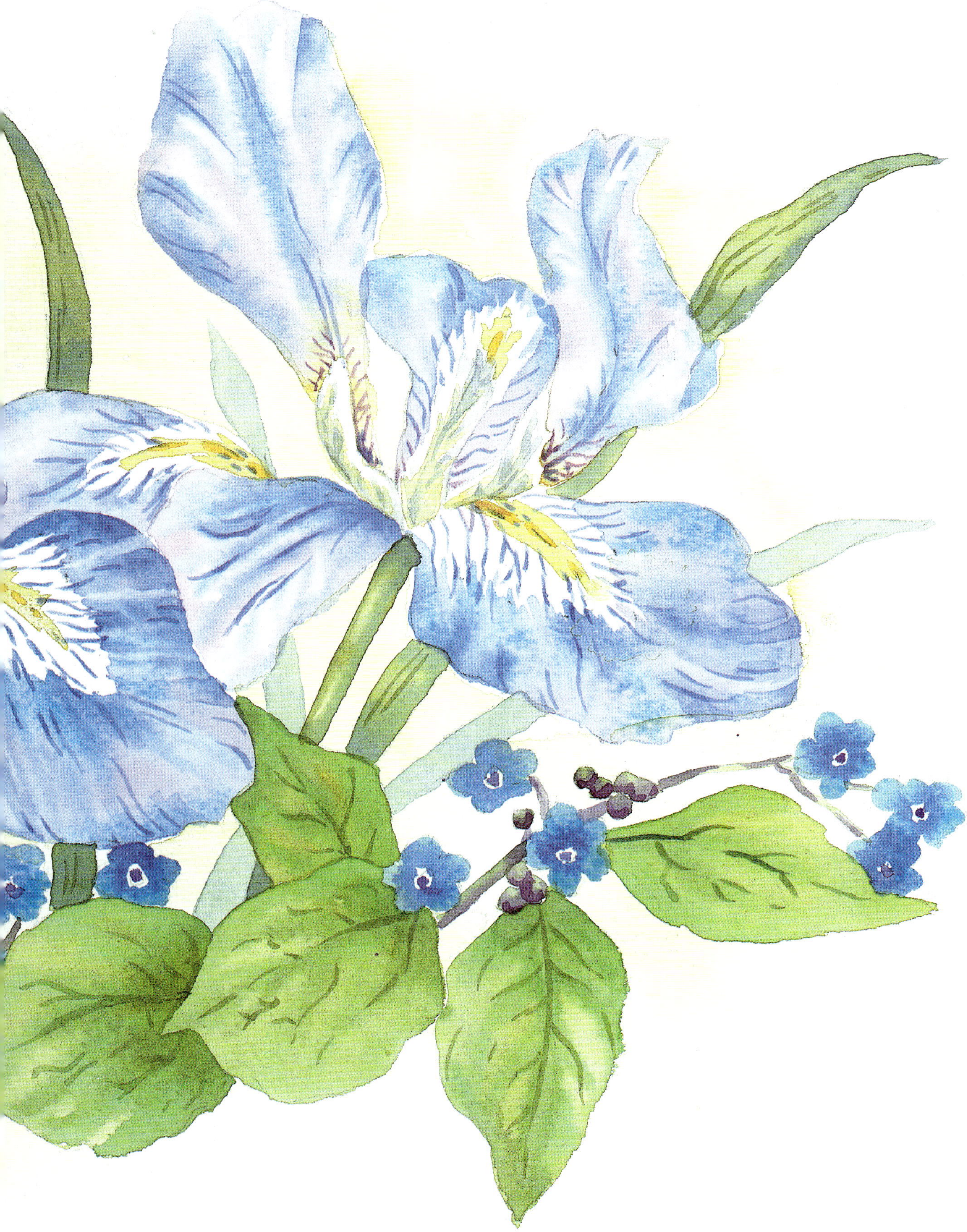

Gold and Rust Iris

TRACING
3

Standing tall in May time, this bi-coloured iris of gold and rust provides a striking subject. To retain a fresh sunny feel, I left a fine gap of white paper surrounding the plant and applied a background wash of aureolin, followed by dilute cobalt blue wet-in-wet to give movement.

Tip

Try to keep your pencil lines light as if you find them hard to remove, they can be particularly visible under yellow.

You will need

- 300gsm (140lb) Not watercolour paper
- Colours: aureolin, new gamboge, raw sienna, cerulean blue, cobalt blue, French ultramarine, alizarin crimson
- Brushes: size 4 round, size 5 round, size 8 round, size 10 round
- Pencils: 2B, H
- Kitchen paper
- Eraser

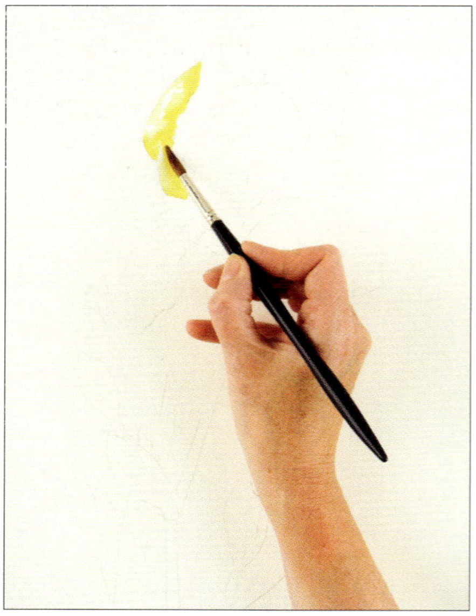

1 Transfer the tracing to your paper following the directions on page 9. Prepare three pools: aureolin, new gamboge and cerulean blue. Using the size 8 round brush loaded with the aureolin, paint in the inner edge of the curled-over section of the top left-hand petal. While still wet, diffuse the colour with water to soften it towards the edge and leave some areas white to suggest highlights.

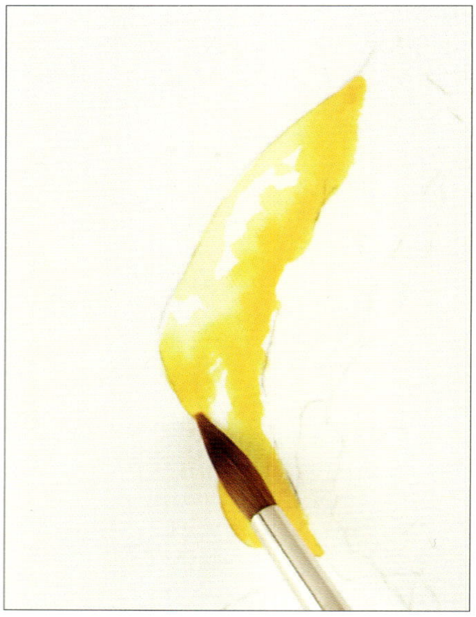

2 While still wet, apply a little new gamboge over the deeper areas to give more depth and form.

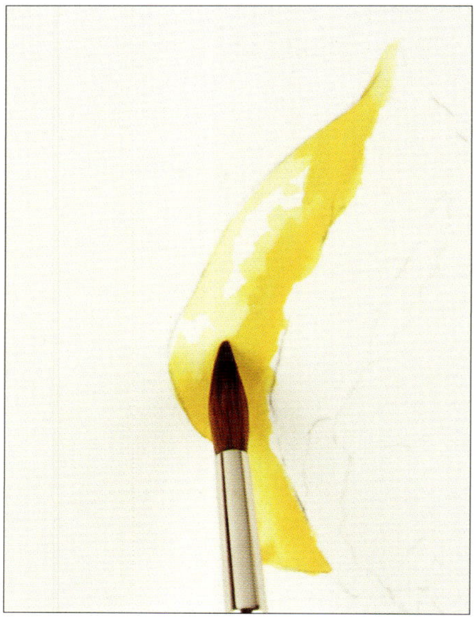

3 Prepare a green-yellow by adding a tiny amount of French ultramarine into the new gamboge. Drop a little of this mix on to the core shadow to accentuate the rounded appearance of this section.

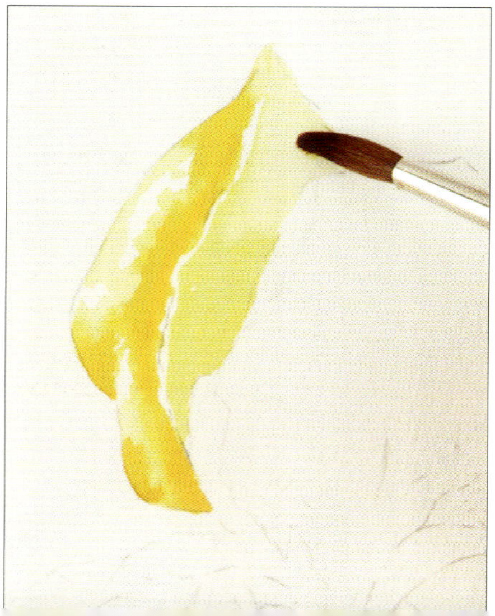

4 Paint in the inside of the petal in fairly dilute aureolin, leaving a fine gap to suggest a highlight on the curved edge. Work from the base upwards, diffusing the colour with water so that it is lighter at the top.

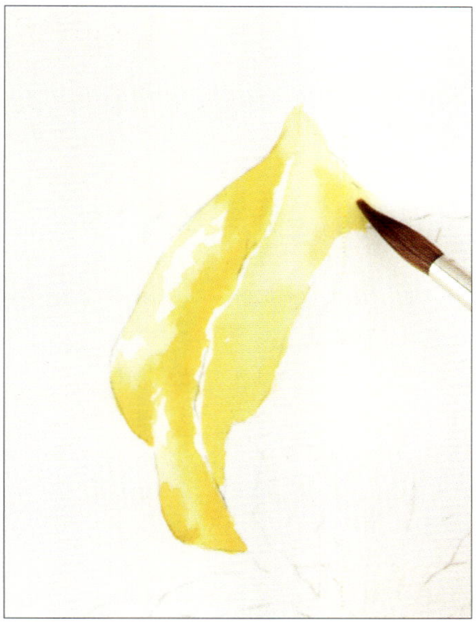

5 Whilst still wet, add in some depth by adding new gamboge at the base and diffuse upwards. Also touch in some colour on to the top right edge.

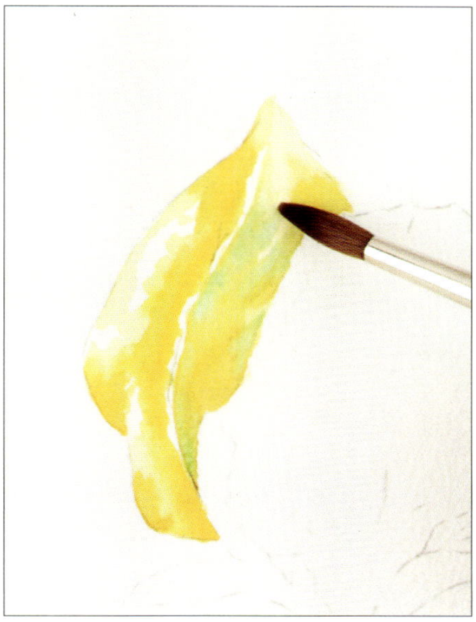

6 Prepare a green mix using new gamboge with a touch of cobalt blue. Apply this quite strongly in the recessed shadowed area and continue whilst wet to drop in a hint of cerulean blue.

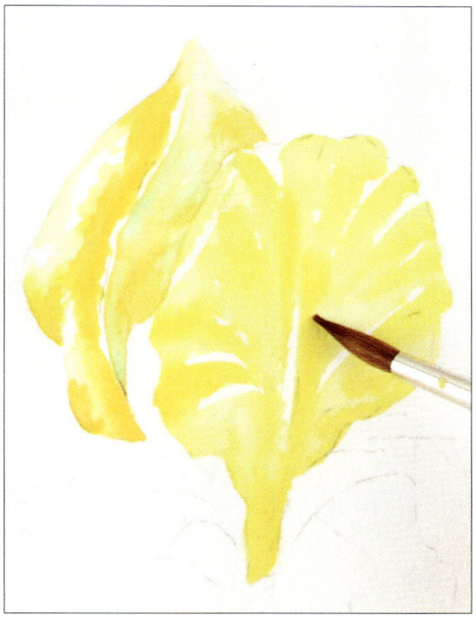

7 Paint in the main top petal using the same method as described in the previous steps. After applying the aureolin wet-on-dry, vary the tone by softening with water. Work from the top and sides of the petal downwards, leaving gaps of white paper to suggest highlights on the petal folds.

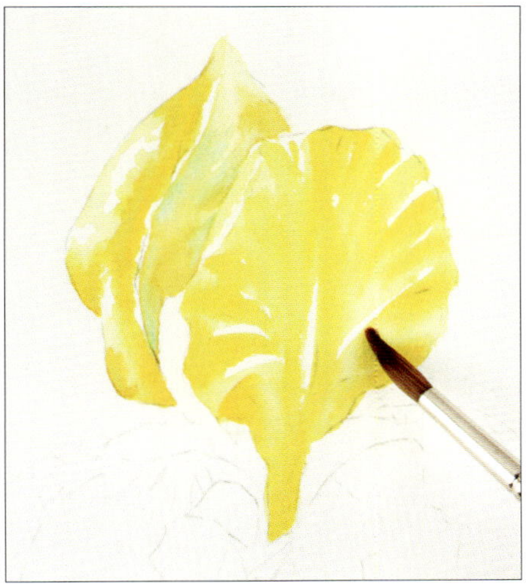

8 While still wet, add in some new gamboge for warmth down the central line and folds of the petal. Apply the green-yellow mix: new gamboge with a touch of French ultramarine while damp to give deeper shadows and definition in the recesses of the folds.

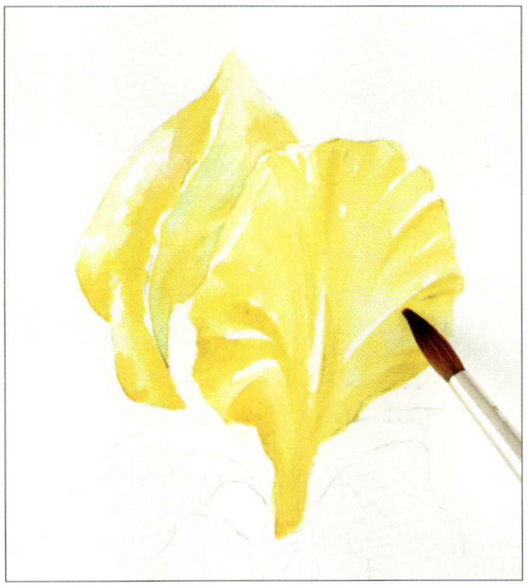

9 To accentuate the shadow under the edge of the petal which is rolling over slightly, dab in a brushstroke of the green used in step 6 and soften with water.

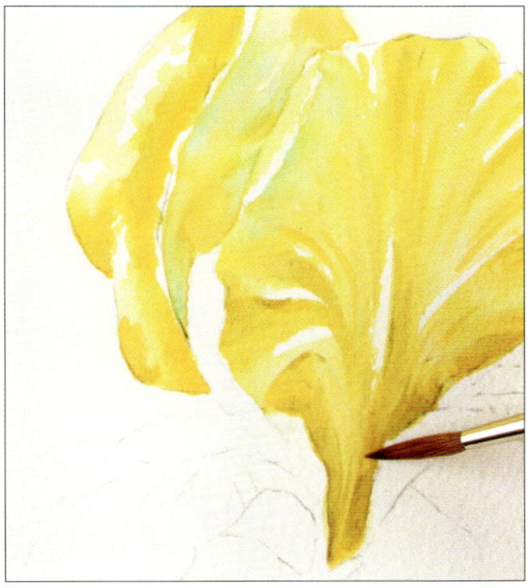

10 Change to a size 5 round brush and, using a stronger mix of green-yellow: new gamboge mixed with a little French ultramarine, paint in the vein details and strengthen the tone towards the base of the petal, softening some of the brushstrokes with water.

Tip

Remember, when you paint wet-on-dry, the colour will appear stronger in tone than the same colour painted on a wet base.

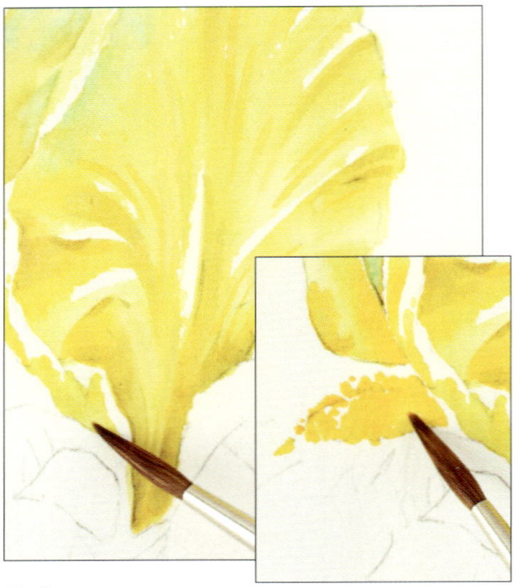

11 Complete the final petal edge and commence on the stamens. Continuing with the size 5 round brush, paint a base wash of new gamboge and stipple the edges using the point of the brush.

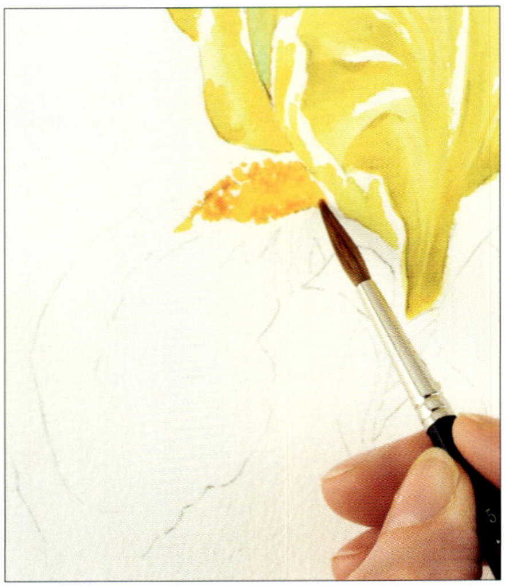

12 Add some alizarin crimson to the pool of new gamboge for warmth. Whilst slightly damp, stipple this mix using the point of your brush. Repeat steps 11 and 12 for the other stamen.

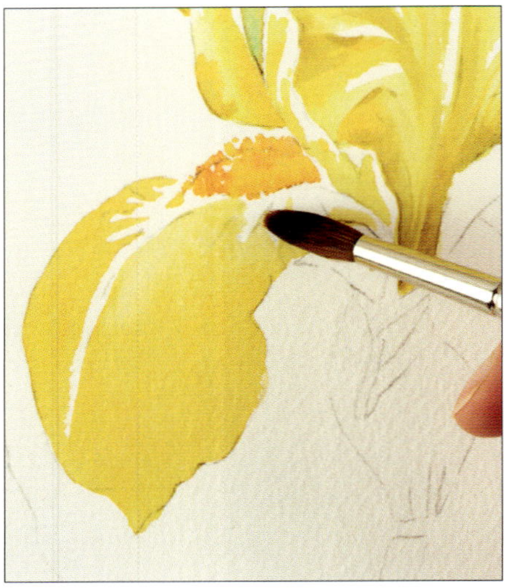

13 Change to a size 8 round brush and prepare a pool of new gamboge and a pool of alizarin crimson to commence on the lower petals. Load your brush with new gamboge and draw the colour from the base upwards, diluting slightly towards the top. Leave a gap of white for the central vein.

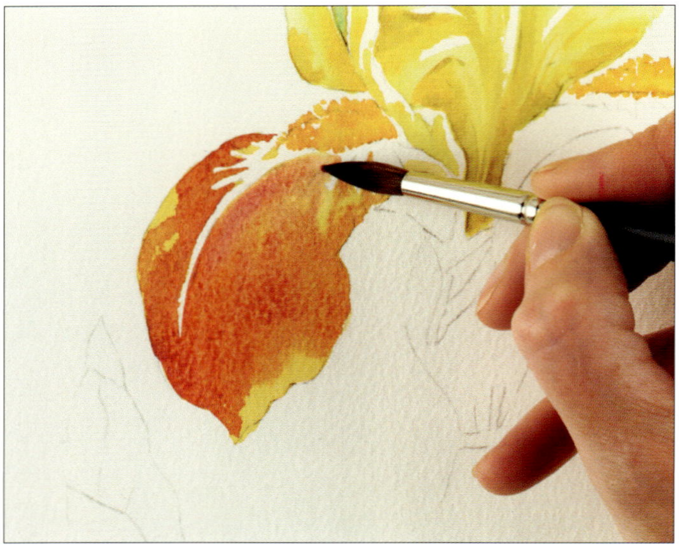

14 While still wet, load your brush with alizarin crimson and run it either side of the white central vein, leaving patches of yellow here and there. Draw the brush upwards to suggest the veins.

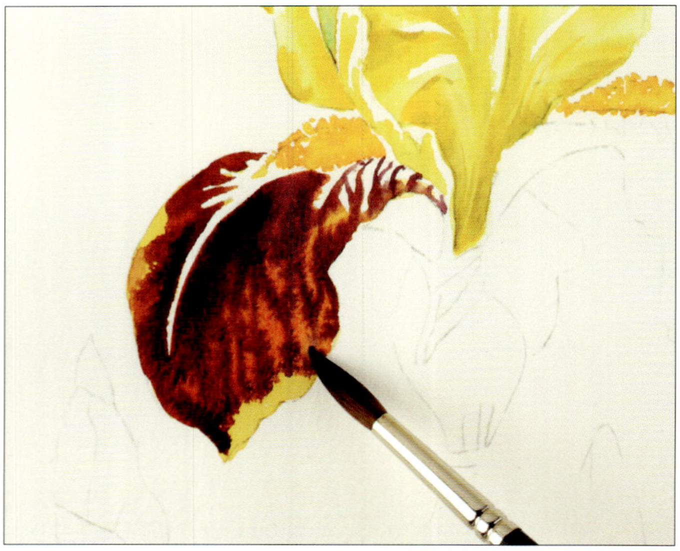

15 Load a stronger mix of alizarin crimson mixed with a tiny amount of French ultramarine on to your brush and apply on top of the previous base while still damp. Work quickly, drawing the colour away from the central vein using the point of the brush to create a diffused colour effect, resulting in a velvety appearance. For added depth, increase the strength of this mix and drop it in wet-on-wet.

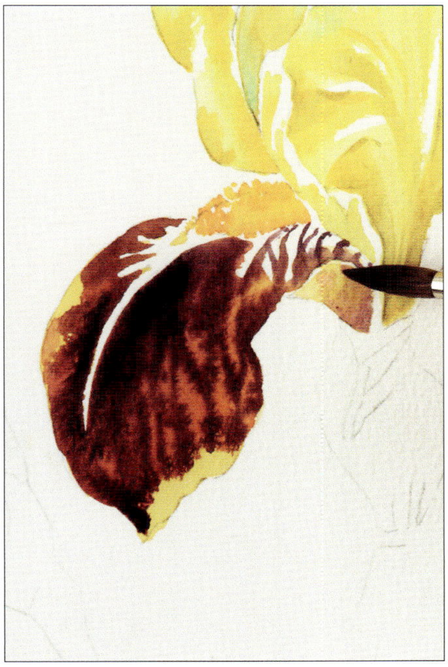

16 Paint the underside of this petal with a base wash of dilute new gamboge. While still wet, draw alizarin crimson upwards and drop in a little of the dilute alizarin crimson and French ultramarine mix. Let the colours flow and blend together. Continue, painting the remaining lower petal to the right plus the middle slightly obscured petal using the same method.

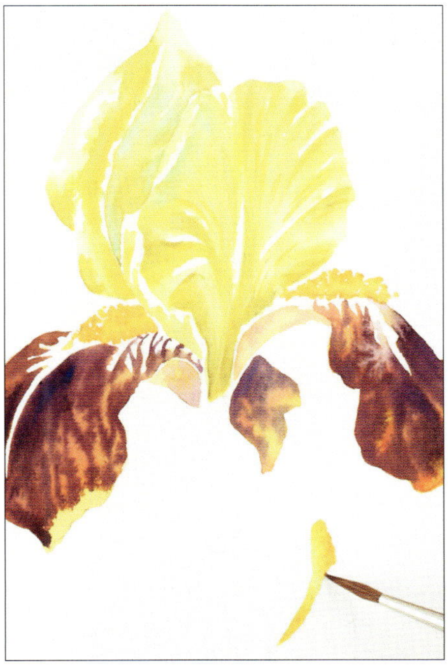

17 For the buds, change to a size 5 round brush and glaze with aureolin. While still damp, run a brushstroke of new gamboge along the shadowed side, the lower recess and the tip. Add further depth in these areas by dropping in a warmer mix of new gamboge with a little alizarin crimson.

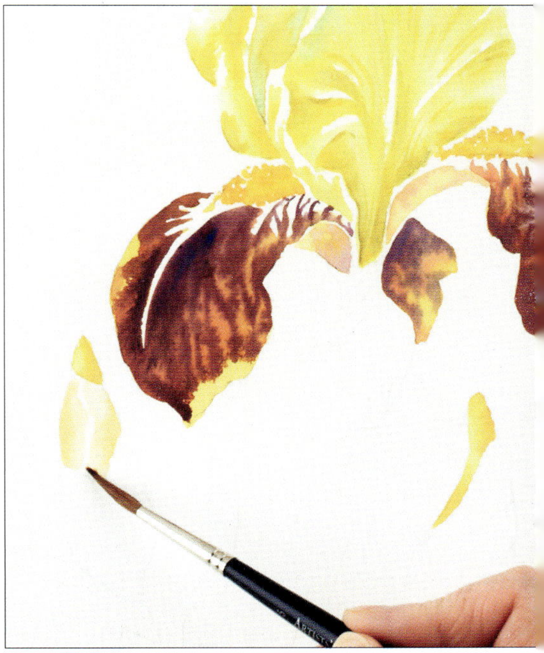

18 For the left-hand bud, paint in the papery covering of the emerging bud with a wash of raw sienna diffused with water. It should be darker along the sides and more dilute towards the centre.

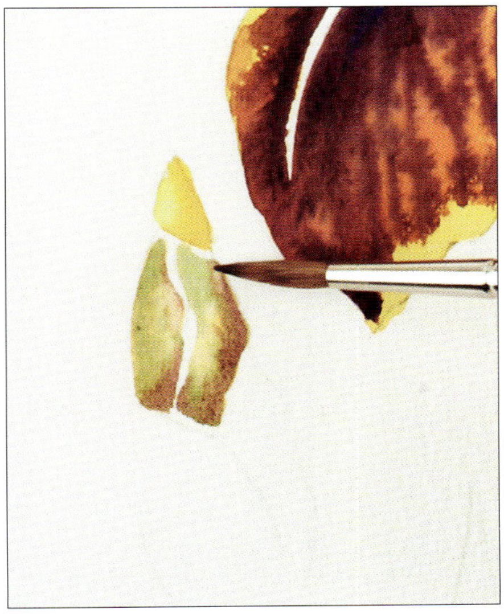

19 While still wet, drop in a yellow-green mix: new gamboge with cobalt blue, followed by a purple-pink mix of alizarin crimson and cobalt blue. Leave to dry.

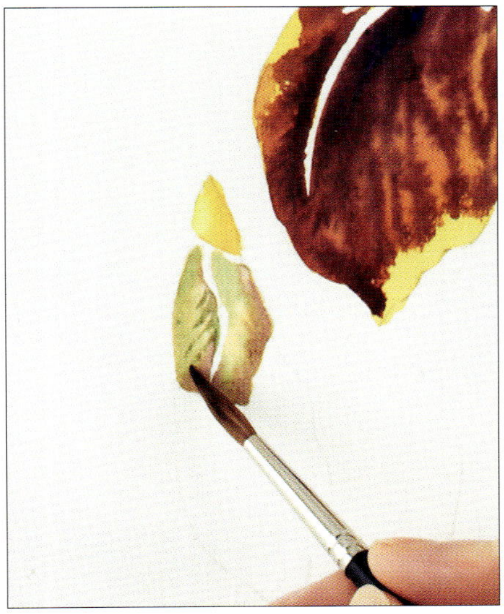

20 Using a stronger mix of the green, sweep the brush at an angle along the edge of the left-hand segment to describe the recesses of the papery surface.

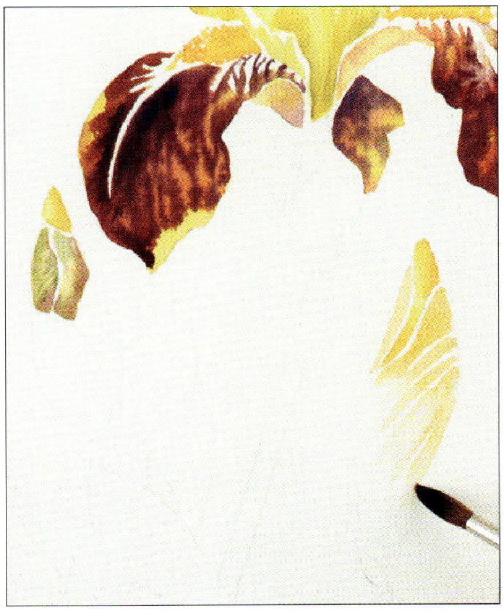

21 For the right-hand bud, change to a size 8 round brush and apply sweeping brushstrokes of raw sienna wet-on-dry, leaving gaps of white paper to suggest the crinkly texture.

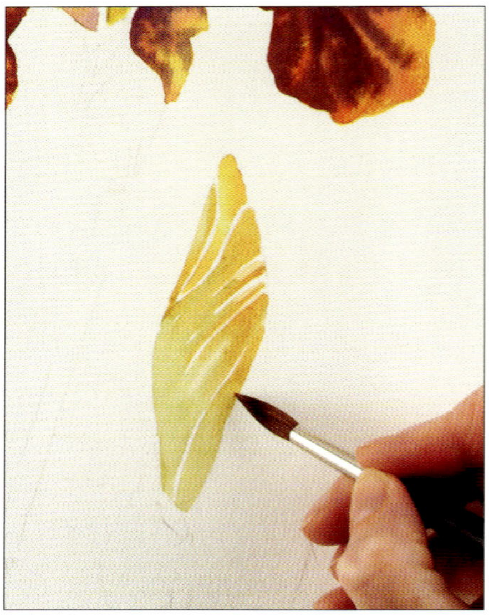

22 While still wet, draw the yellow-green mix from the left-hand edge upwards so as to merge with the raw sienna, followed by a stronger mix of raw sienna on the right-hand side of the bud sweeping downwards. Leave to dry.

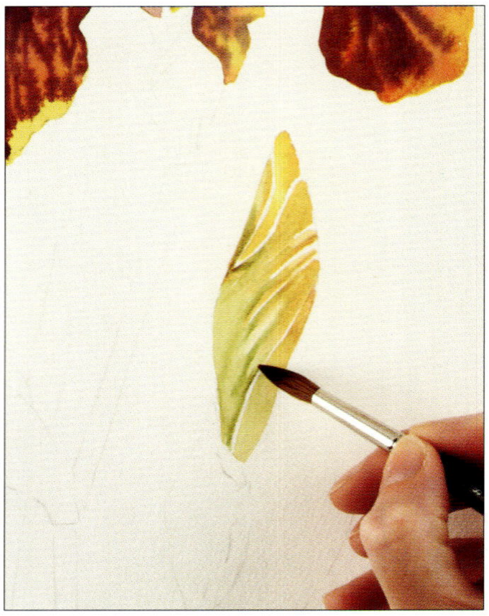

23 When dry, add deeper tones of green over the left-hand side of the bud and a purple-pink mix in the recesses over the raw sienna. Soften slightly with water.

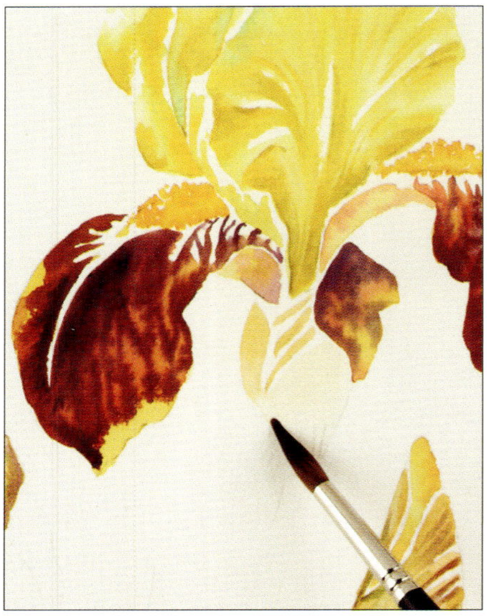

24 Continuing on the base (ovary) of the top flower head, apply three short brushstrokes of raw sienna to suggest the papery folds and work from the left-hand side downwards with full strength before softening with water over the remaining area.

Tip

If the paint starts to dry when you are working wet-in-wet, let it dry thoroughly first and then re-wet using a brush dipped in clean water.

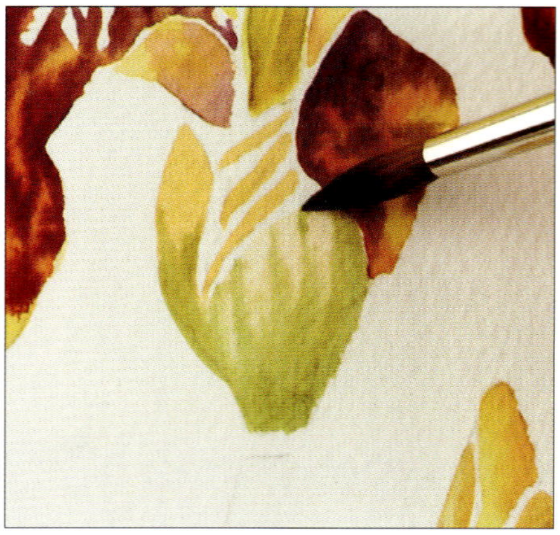

25 While still damp, apply the yellow-green mix from the base upwards, leaving gaps to reveal the raw sienna wash underneath.

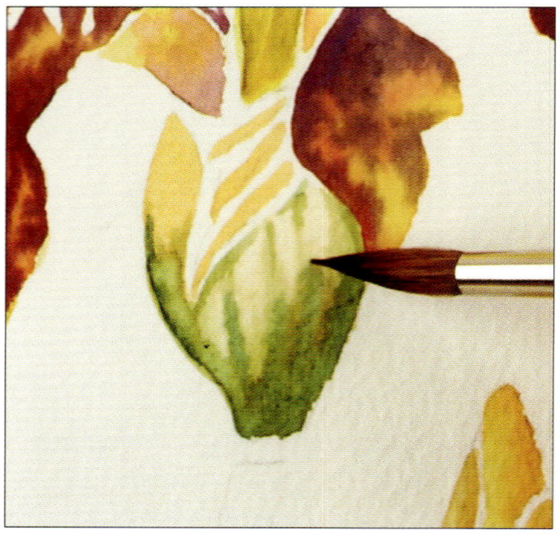

26 Make a blue-green mix: French ultramarine with a little new gamboge to make a mid-tone shade of green, and add more brushstrokes on top, working from the base upwards. Leave to dry.

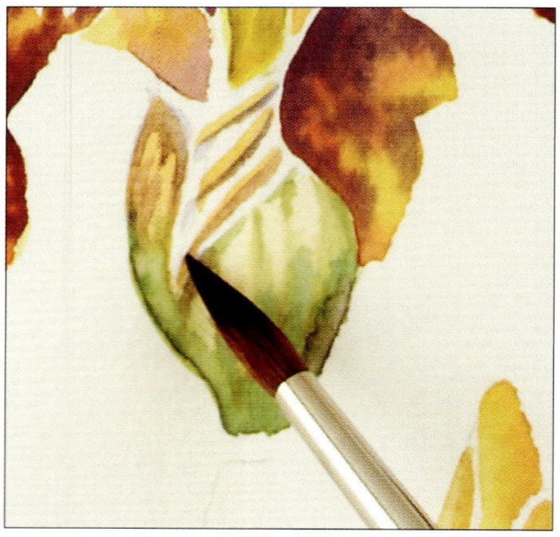

27 Apply the purple-pink mix with sweeping brushstrokes under the raw sienna lines and to the left-hand side to give more depth.

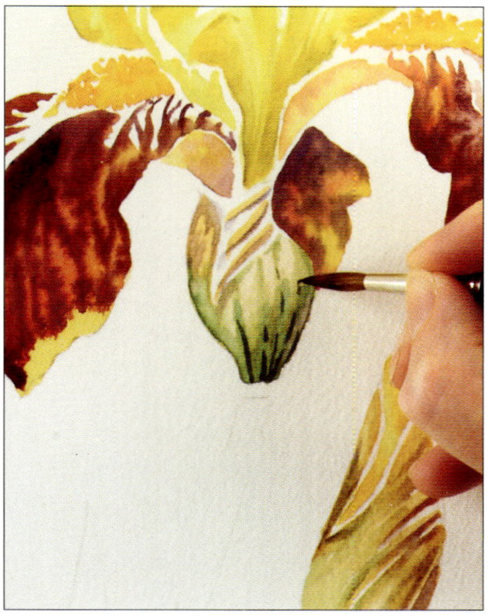

28 Make a stronger shade of green using equal parts of new gamboge and French ultramarine. Using a size 5 round brush, work from the base upwards, wet-on-dry, adding broken lines to describe the veins and shape.

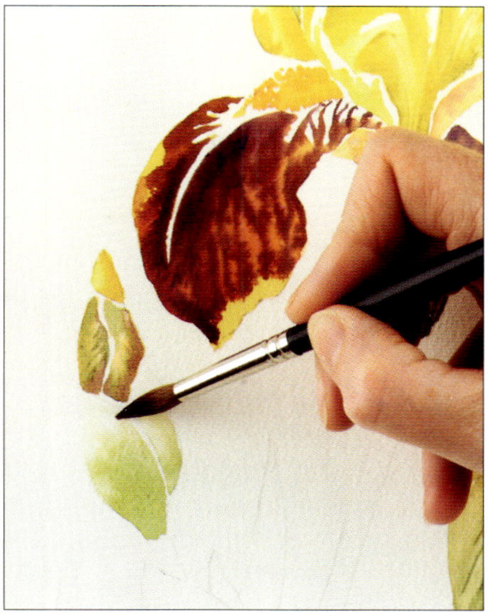

29 Return to a size 8 round brush to work on the lower half of the left-hand bud. Work the yellow-green mix upwards and diffuse with water to cover the top half.

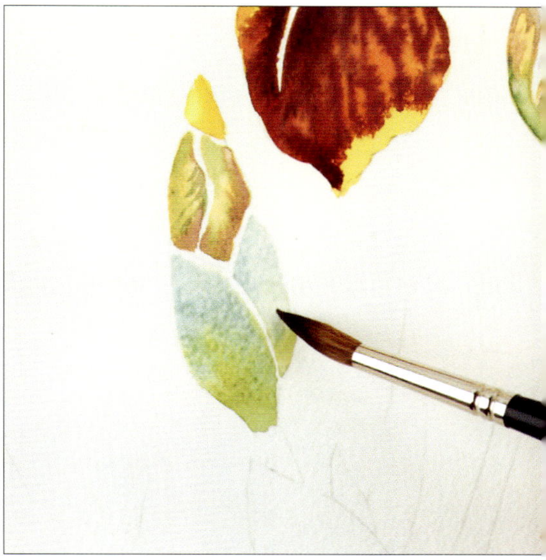

30 While wet, apply the blue-green mix from the top of this section of the bud downwards to bleed down into the yellow-green. Leave to dry slightly.

Tip

On a separate sheet of paper, test your colour mixes and washes to ensure you have the right shade. Try to get into the habit of recording every colour you mix, then you will have a colour swatch for reference.

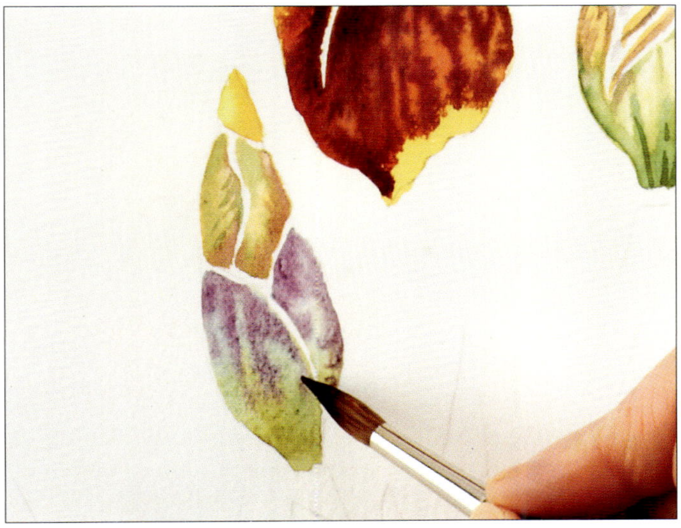

31 While slightly damp, using the purple-pink mix of alizarin crimson and French ultramarine, pull the colour downwards. Allow the colours to bleed freely into each other and leave gaps to reveal the colours underneath. Repeat steps 29–31 for the other two buds and leave to dry.

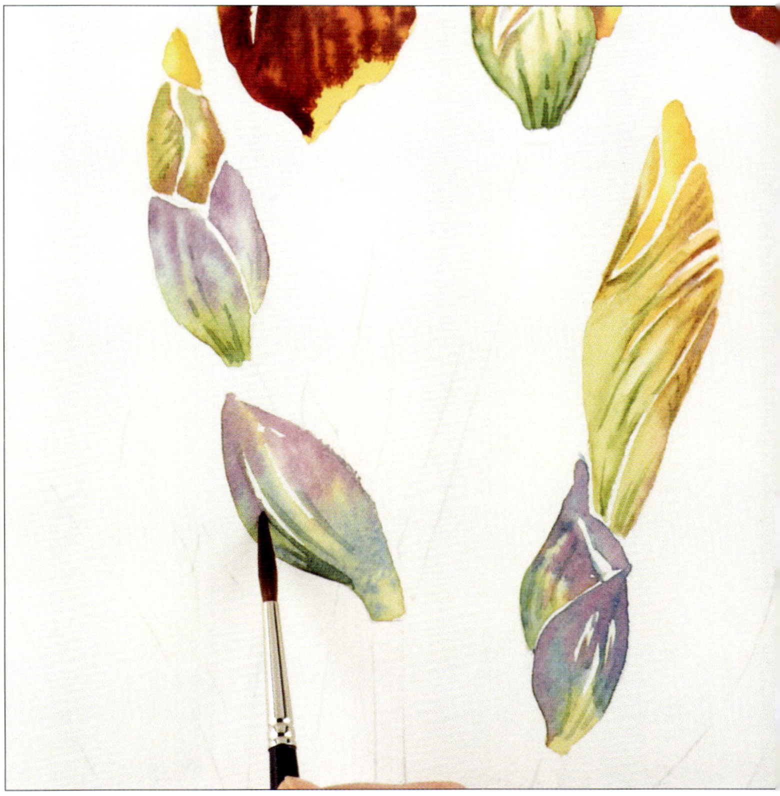

32 Add a little alizarin crimson to the green used in step 28 to make a richer green and, using a size 5 round brush, add in a few veins on each bud when dry, working from the base upwards.

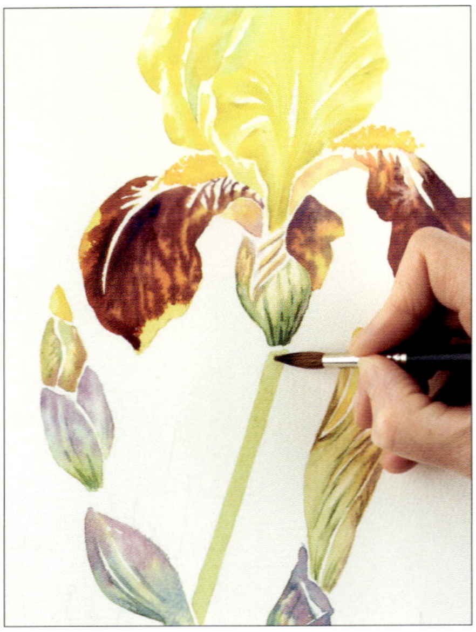

33 For the stems, change to a size 8 round brush and, using the yellow-green mix, work your brush in sections from bottom to top, leaving a small white gap between the top of the stem and the bud.

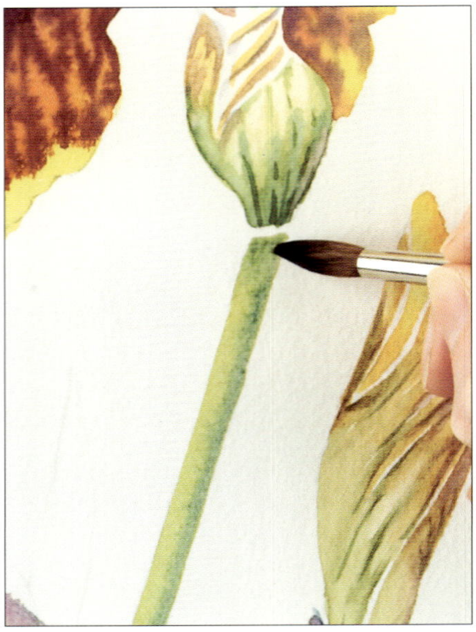

34 Whilst still damp, apply the blue-green mix from the base upwards using quick strokes along the right-hand shadowed side. Allow the colours to blend. This will add depth and a sense of roundness to the stem.

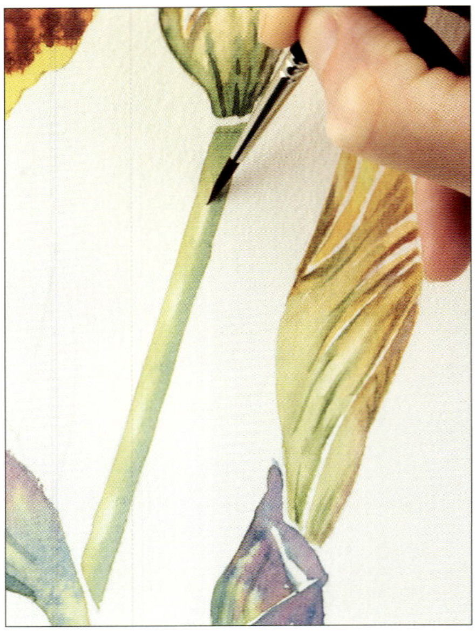

35 Take a clean, damp size 4 round brush. Lift out a few highlights on the left of the stem, working from the bottom to the top in a broken line. Repeat steps 33–35 for the other stems.

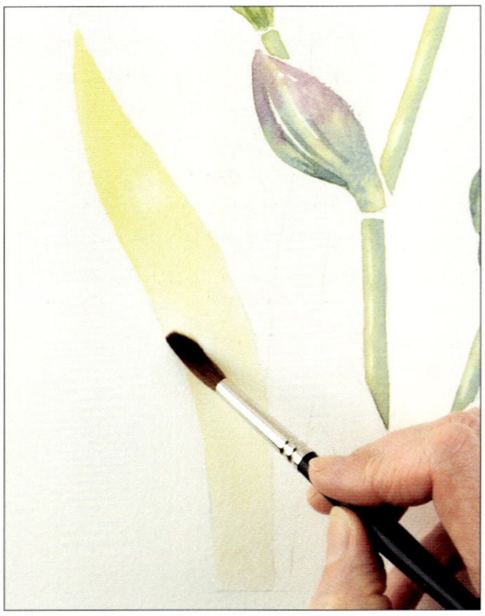

36 For the leaves, return to the size 8 round brush. Prepare three pools of colour: new gamboge, cobalt blue and a combination of the two. Starting with new gamboge at the tip, pull the colour downwards and soften by adding water until the lower part is merely a glaze of water.

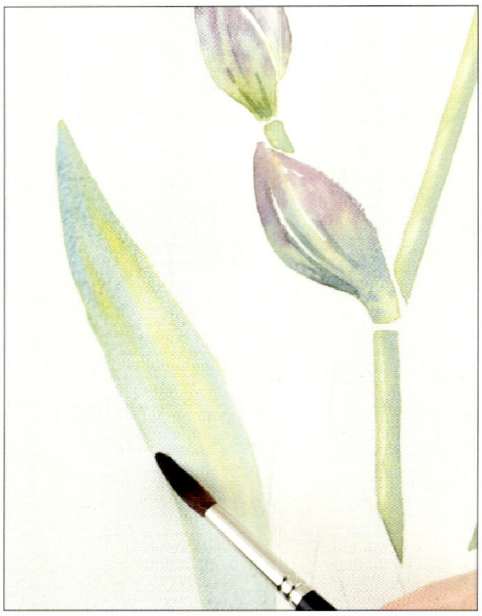

37 Load your brush with dilute cobalt blue. Work brushstrokes from both the tip downwards and the base upwards to create a soft wet-in-wet blend of colour.

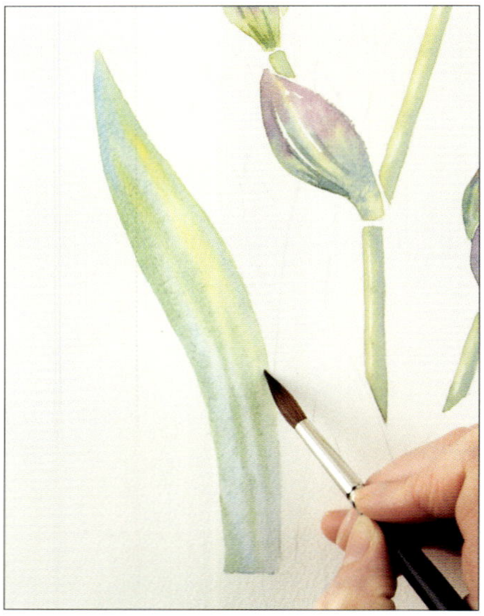

38 While still wet, use the green mix to add in the soft veins. Repeat steps 36–38 for the other yellow-green leaf.

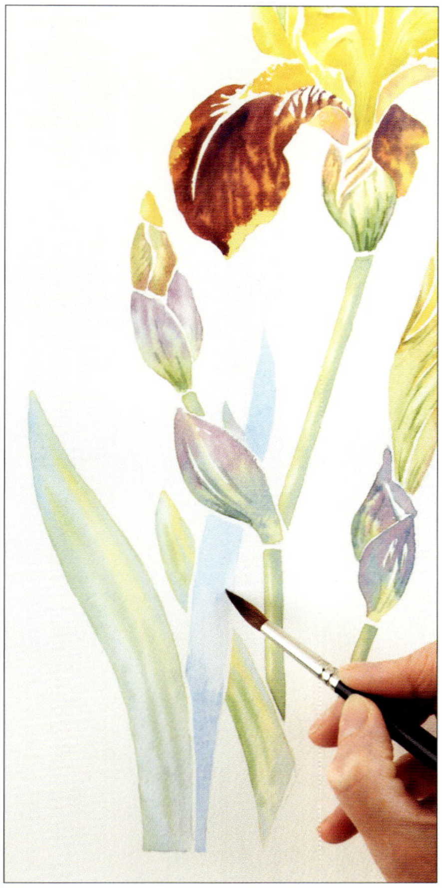

39 To add variety the remaining leaves have a blue base. Apply a neat pale wash of cobalt blue working from the tip downwards. Vary the tone by adding water.

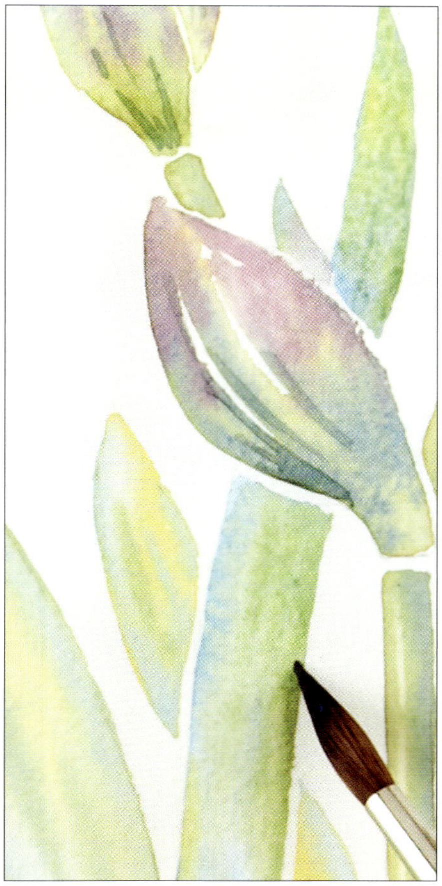

40 While wet, apply new gamboge from the tip of the leaf downwards, allowing the colours to merge, creating a shade of green. Add sweeping strokes of the green mix to suggest veins. Repeat steps 39 and 40 for the remaining leaves and allow to dry.

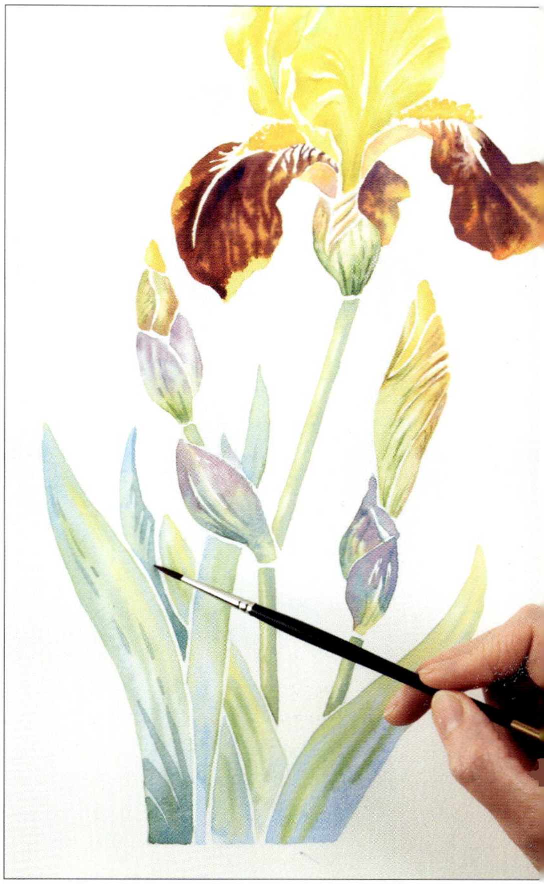

41 Prepare a blue-green mix of French ultramarine and new gamboge with a dash of alizarin crimson. Add in the shadows and vein details using a size 8 round brush, but you may want to use a size 5 round for the finer details. Where the leaves overlap, add shadow to the leaf underneath. Repeat this stage for all of the leaves. Make sure the paint is thoroughly dry, and using a clean, hard eraser, remove all the pencil lines.

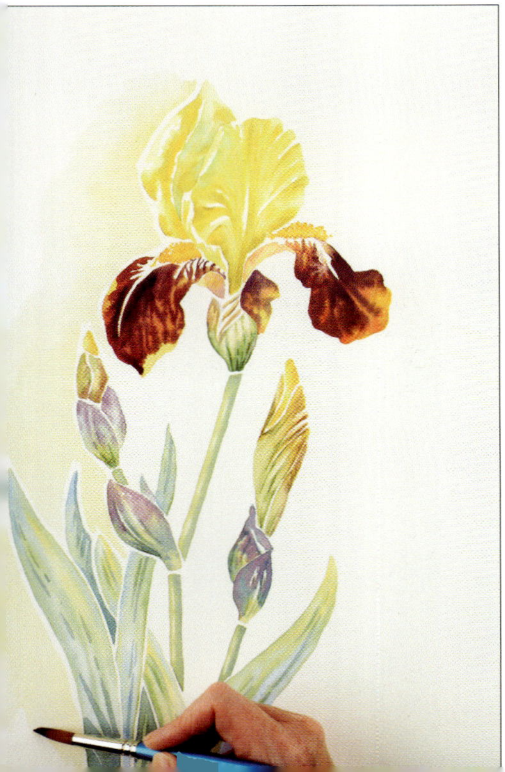

42 Prepare a dilute pool of aureolin. Using a size 10 round brush apply the wash to the background, working in sections from the top downwards. Leave a loose white edge around the flowers and leaves to give the painting a light, fresh appearance and soften the outer edges of the wash.

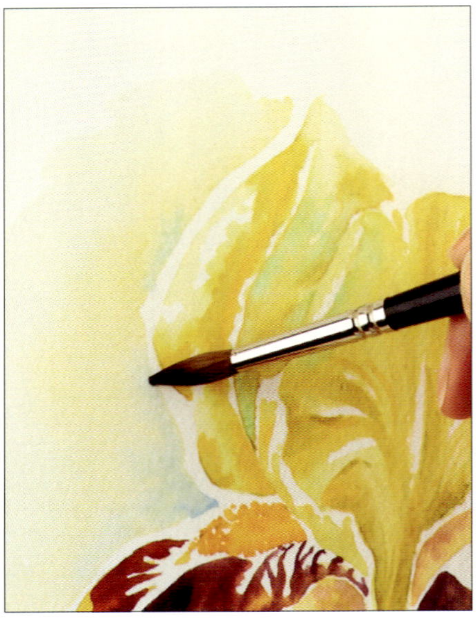

43 While each section is still damp, use the point of a size 8 round brush to drop in dilute cobalt blue around some of the edges.

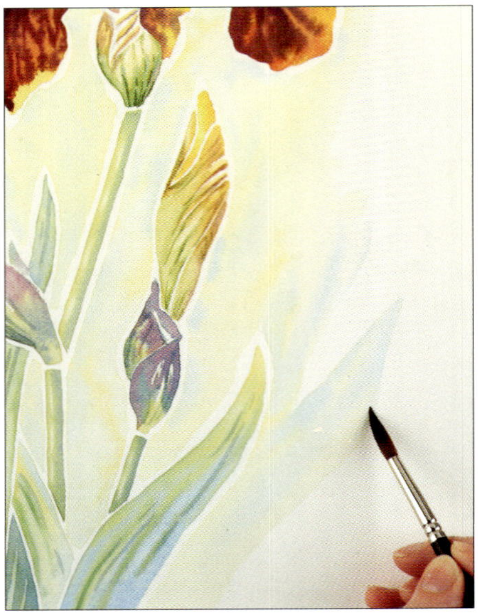

44 Continue with steps 42–44 until the background is covered. Add a few wet-in-wet suggestions of leaves using pale cobalt blue. For the far right section of the background, follow the suggested outline of the silhouette of a leaf.

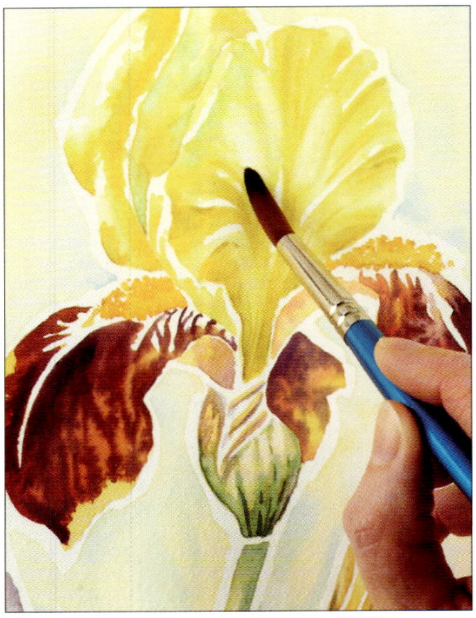

45 Observe your painting to check if you need more highlights, depth or detail. To lift out highlights, use a brush dipped in a little clean water and dab out the colour.

Tip

You can use whatever size brush you feel is appropriate for the area you are working on when lifting out highlights. In step 45, Julie used a size 10 round brush.

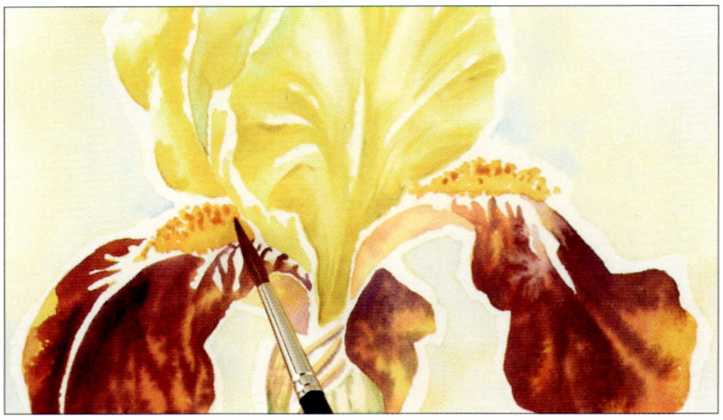

46 To add in a little more detail to the stamen, use a size 5 round brush and stipple on a mix of alizarin crimson and new gamboge. Stipple using the point of your brush to add texture and definition.

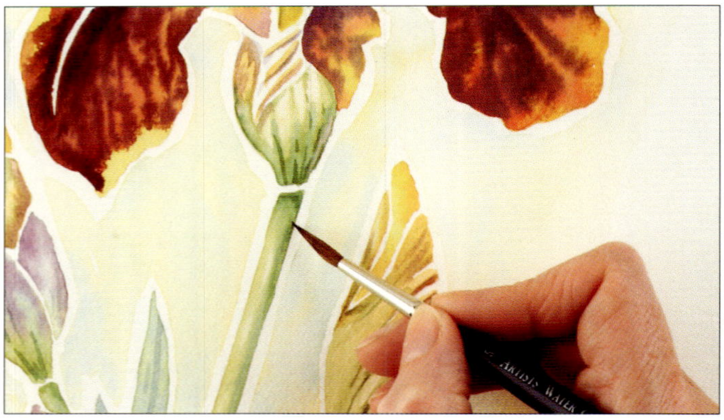

47 Finally, using the strong mix of equal parts of French ultramarine and new gamboge deepen the top and the base of the stem. Apply the colour wet-on-dry and diffuse. If the shadowed side of the stems need more strength, run a loaded brush along the side and again soften with water. Leave to dry and remove any pencil lines with a clean eraser.

Opposite

The finished painting, reduced in size.

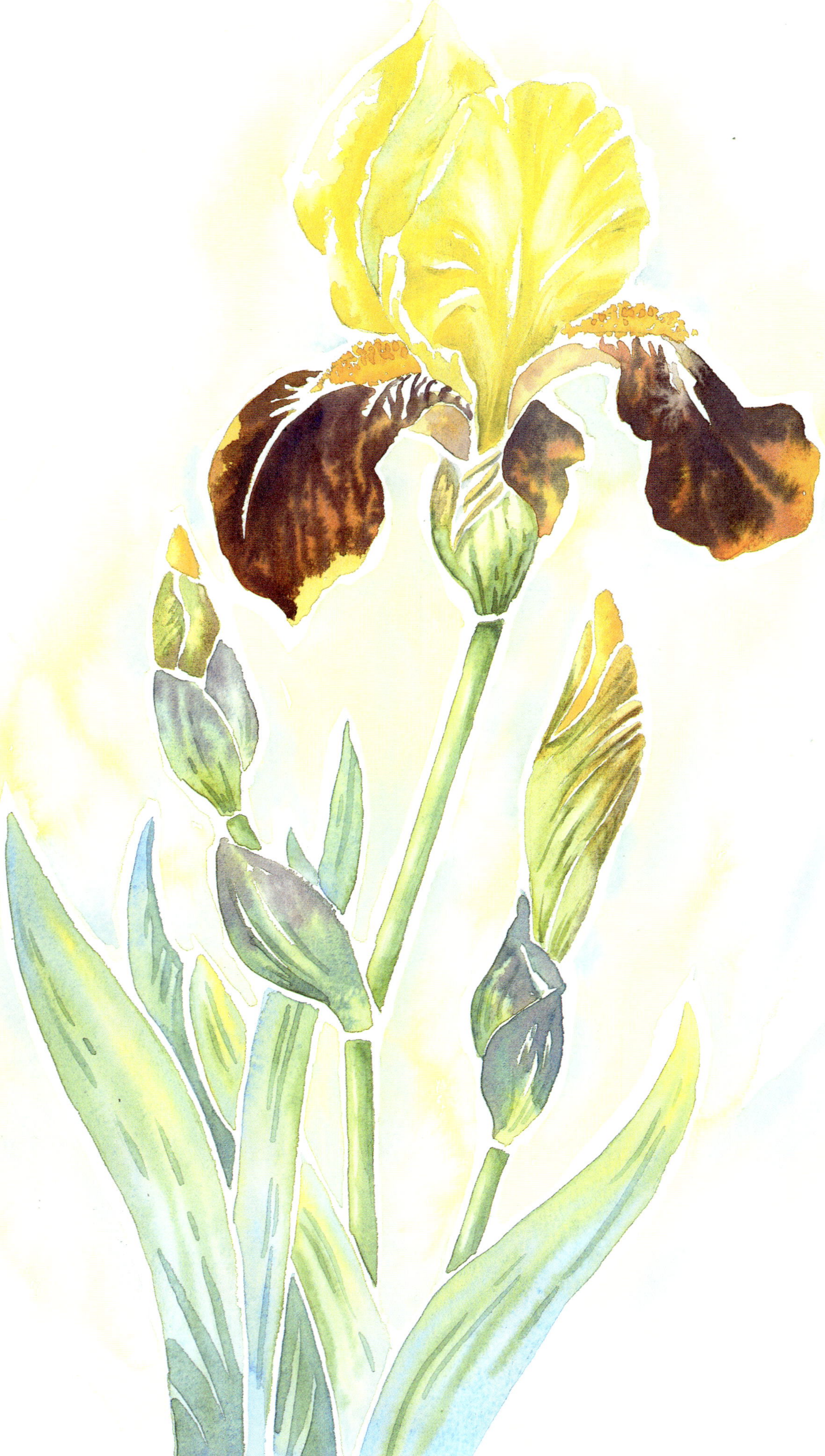

Deep Purple Irises

TRACING 4

These beautiful purple irises appear both elegant and strong. The challenge of painting them was to capture the feel of the velvety lower petals and the fragile, tissue paper appearance of the paler top petals. The crumpled papery coverings from which the buds emerge add an extra element to this composition.

You will need

300gsm (140lb) Not watercolour paper

Colours: aureolin, new gamboge, Indian yellow, raw sienna, cerulean blue, cobalt blue, French ultramarine, indigo, quinacridone magenta, alizarin crimson

Brushes: size 4 round, size 5 round, size 8 round, size 10 round, size 12 round

Pencils: 2B, H

Kitchen paper

Eraser

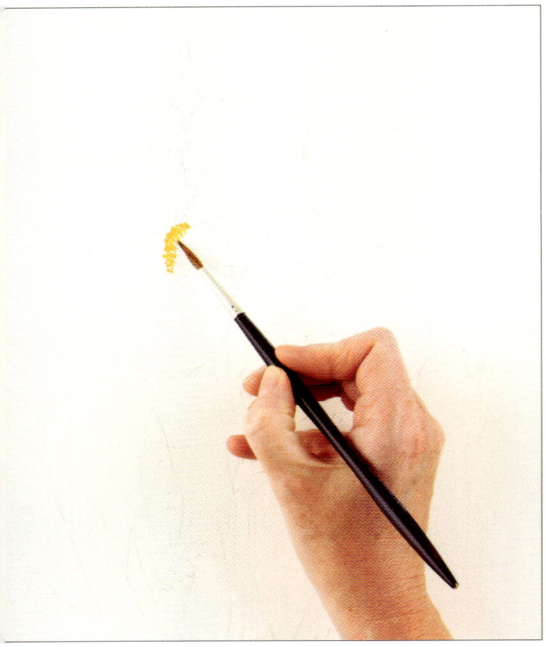

1 Transfer the tracing to your paper following the instructions on page 9. Prepare a pool of Indian yellow and, using a size 5 round brush, stipple on the colour and then draw it down slightly to suggest the tiny filaments supporting the stamens.

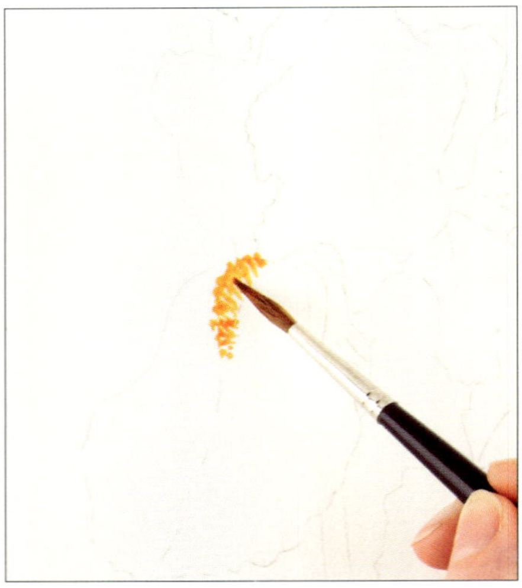

2 While still damp, add a touch of quinacridone magenta to the yellow and, using the point of your brush, drop the colour in and let it bleed down the lines.

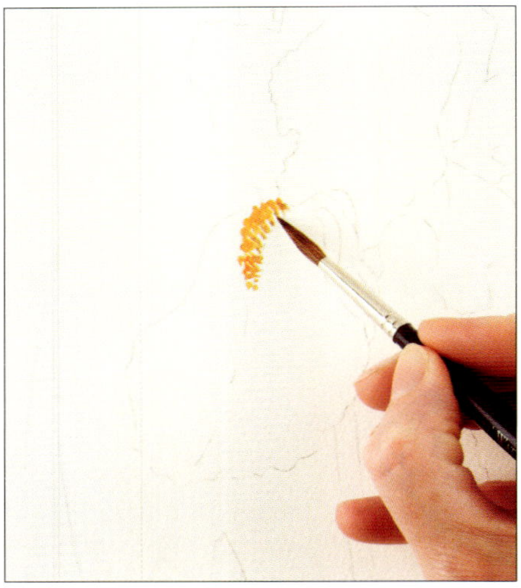

3 Prepare a mauve mix of alizarin crimson and French ultramarine. Drop a little of this colour on to the base of the stamens. Repeat these steps for all of the stamens.

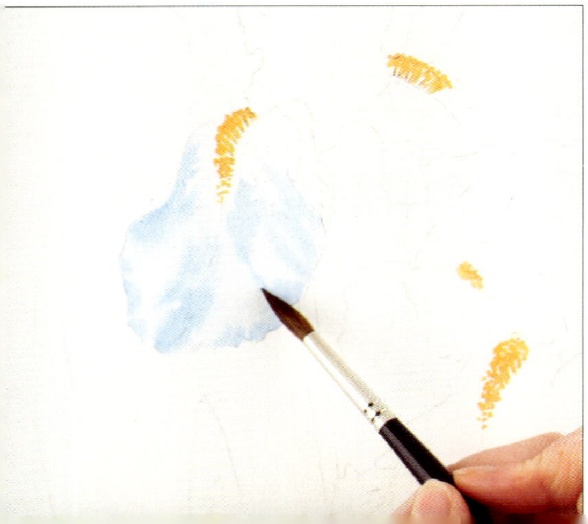

4 Prepare a pool of dilute cobalt blue and a pink-purple mix of quinacridone magenta with French ultramarine with. Glaze the lower left petal of the top flower with the pale cobalt, pulling the wash from the sides and base inwards and tapering it off to fine lines to suggest the veins surrounding the stamen. Add more pigment to the cobalt blue mix and drop this into the damp base to add depth and form.

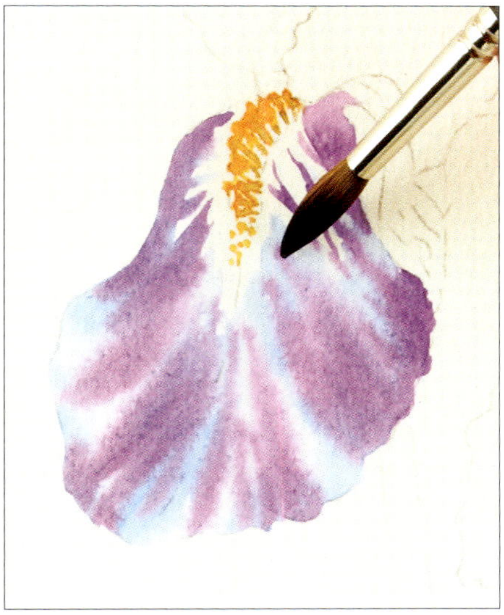

5 While still wet, work the pink-purple mix into the base wash. Pull the brushstrokes in from the edge with a sweeping movement, again letting the colour taper into the veins. Leave to dry thoroughly.

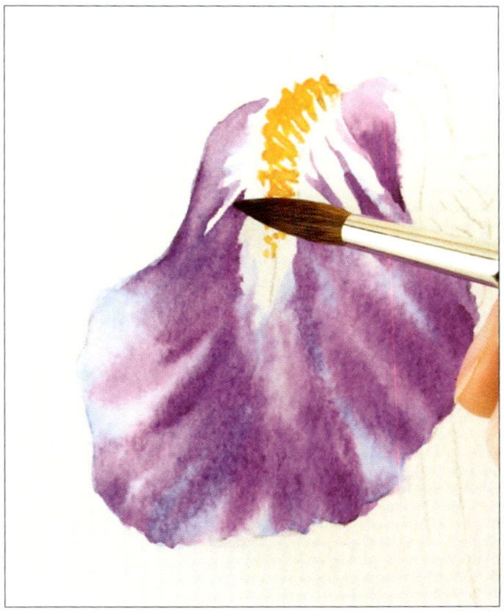

6 Strengthen the pink-purple mix and glaze the petal with water. Add stronger sweeping brushstrokes from the base upwards to give depth and a suggestion of the deeper recesses of the petal folds. Touch the edges here and there to describe the fluted edges.

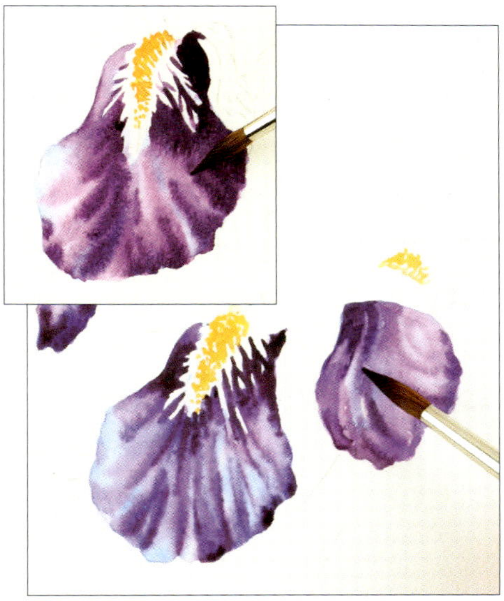

7 Prepare a mix of alizarin crimson and indigo and quickly apply in the same way as before on the damp base. If the paint has dried, re-wet with water and continue. Repeat steps 4–7 on the remaining lower petals. Vary the proportions of colour in the mixes to add variety. Leave to dry.

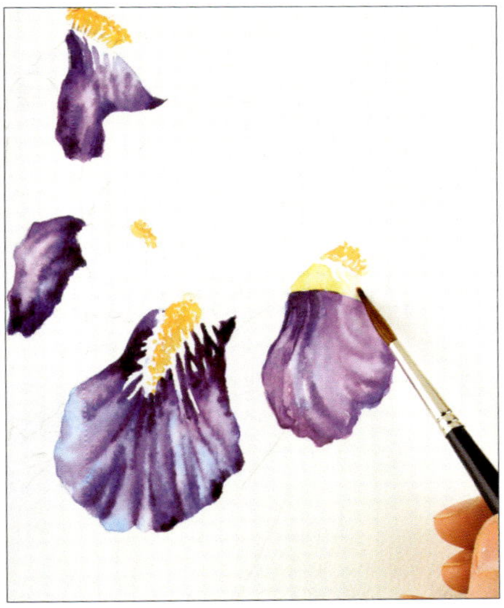

8 Prepare a pool of pale new gamboge and apply it to the top edge of the right-hand lower petal. Draw the colour up towards the stamens.

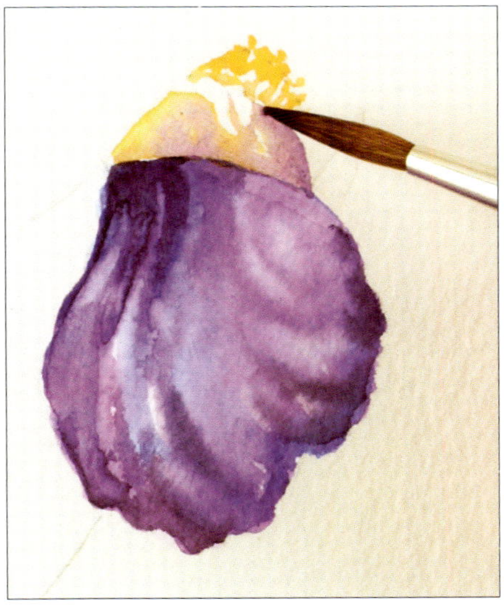

9 Mix quinacridone magenta and French ultramarine together. Whilst the base is still damp, run the colour along the lower edge of the petal so that it bleeds upwards into the yellow.

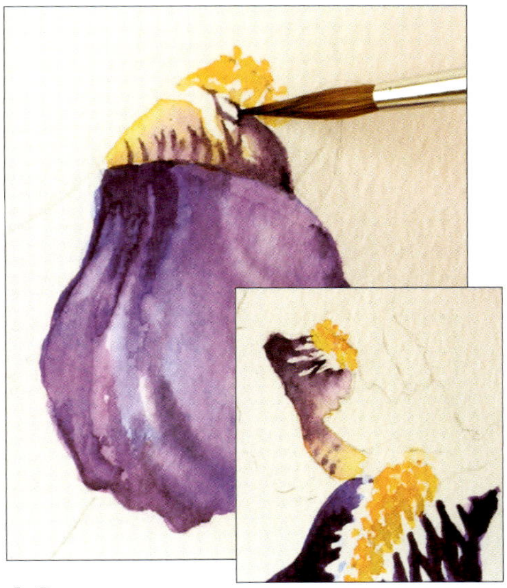

10 Using the alizarin crimson and indigo mix, draw the point of the brush upwards while it is damp to suggest veins. Repeat steps 8–10 in a similar way on the remaining top section of the petal on the same bloom (tucked behind the small inner petals).

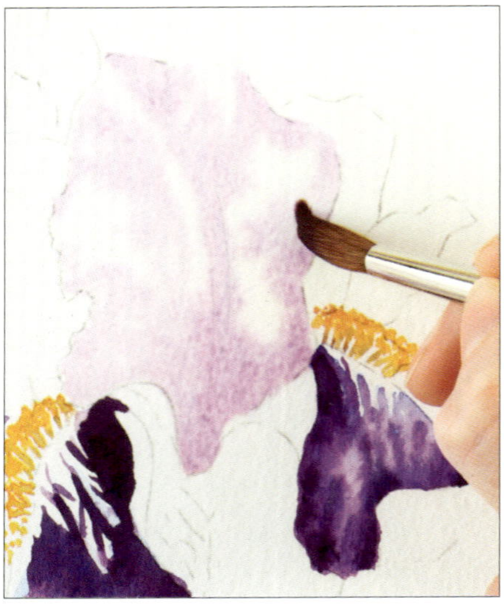

11 Prepare a fresh pink-mauve pool of colour: quinacridone magenta plus cobalt blue. Using a size 8 round brush, glaze the top central petal with water. Pull the colour from the base upwards along the central vein and towards the sides, leaving white areas.

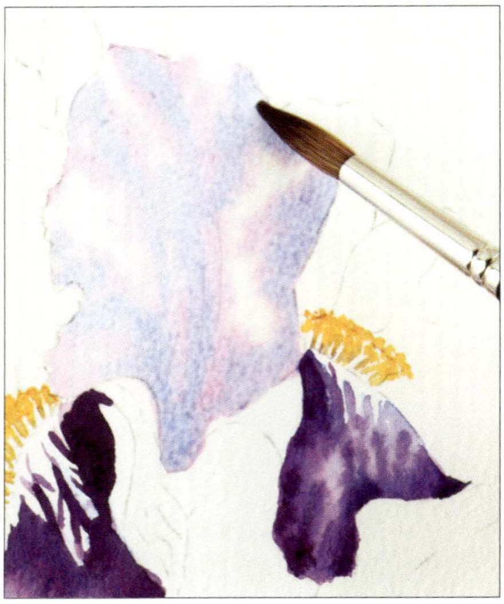

12 While wet, sweep in brushstrokes of dilute cobalt blue on top of the mauve and drop in colour at the edges. Allow the colours to blend together.

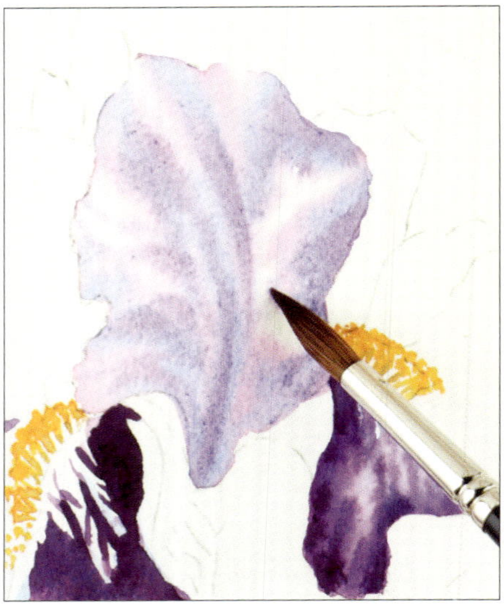

13 Increase the strength of the mauve mix. While the petal is still damp, work from the base upwards in this stronger shade to add depth and apply curved brushstrokes from the edges inwards to describe the folds of the petal. Leave to dry slightly.

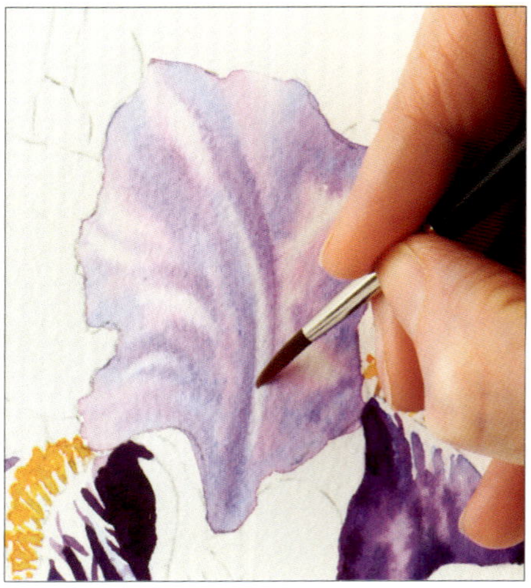

14 Change to a size 4 round brush and lift out some highlights on the petal where the light catches it. Leave to dry.

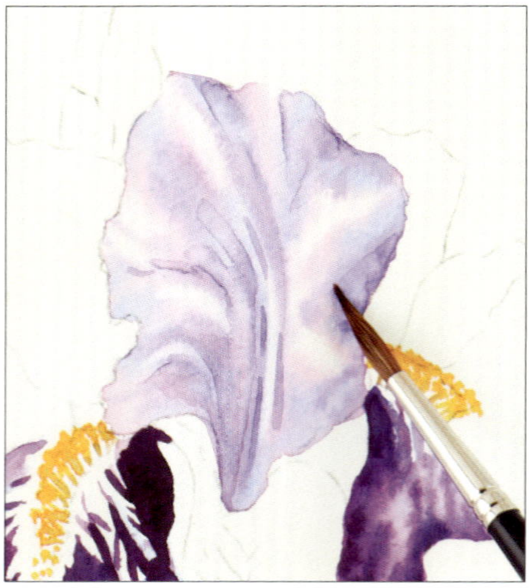

15 Prepare a slightly stronger mix of quinacridone magenta and French ultramarine, using proportionally more of the blue shade in the mix. Working wet-on-dry, add deeper brushstrokes surrounding the central light vein and on the edges to accentuate the shadowed areas of the folds. Soften a few hard edges with water. Repeat steps 11–15 on the petals either side and on the lower flower head.

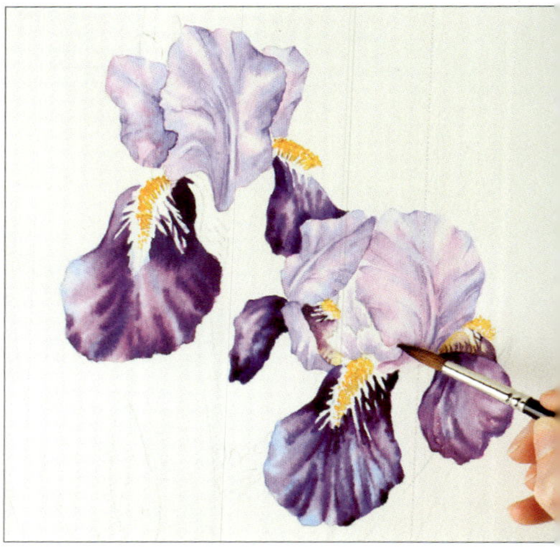

16 Change to a size 8 round brush and prepare two pale mixes: a pink-mauve using predominantly quinacridone magenta and a touch of cobalt blue and a blue-mauve using French ultramarine and a dash of quinacridone magenta. Work wet-on-dry on the three small, serrated-edge inner petals of the right-hand bloom with the pink-mauve mix first. Starting with the petal behind, draw the brush along the serrated edge of the two in front, pulling the colour upwards in the direction of its curve. Diffuse with water and leave a white edge.

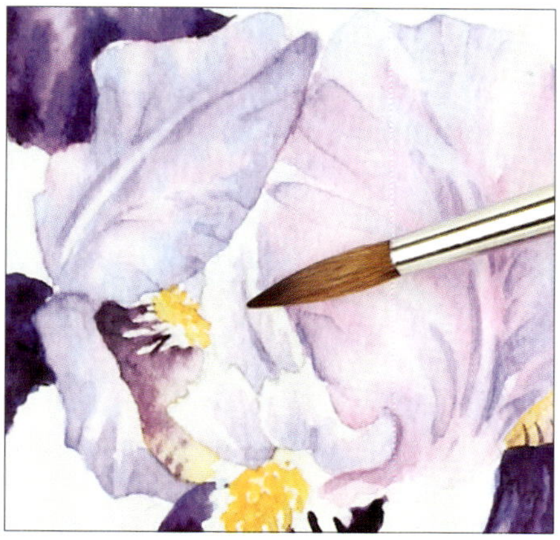

17 While still wet, drop in a little of the blue-mauve mix at the base of each petal. Let it flow into the base colour, leaving some white around the edge of the petal. Leave to dry. Add a central vein using the blue-mauve shade.

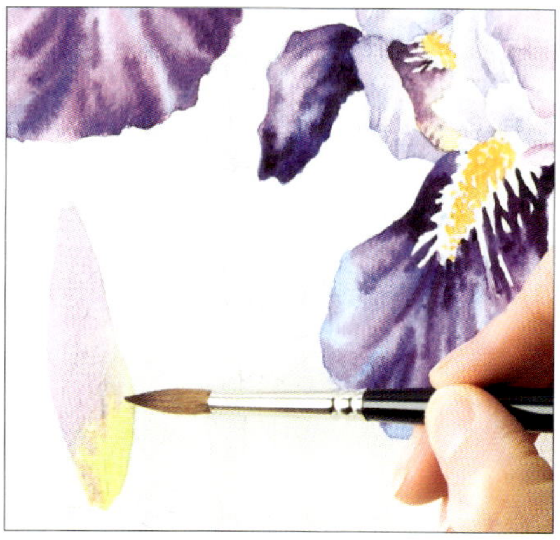

18 Work on the buds wet-on-dry. Prepare three mixes: aureolin with a touch of cerulean blue to make a cool yellow-green, quinacridone magenta with cobalt blue (fairly strong) to make a pink-mauve and French ultramarine with quinacridone magenta to make a blue-mauve. Load your brush with the yellow-green and work from the base of the lower bud upwards in sweeping strokes. Take the pink-mauve and work from the tip downwards so that the two colours meet and merge together slightly.

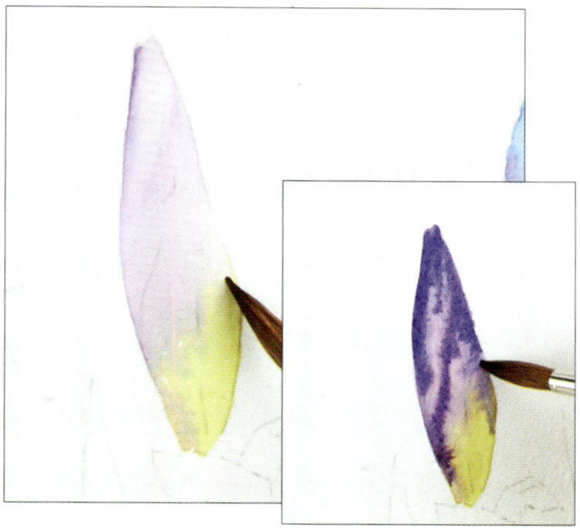

19 While still wet, apply the strong blue-mauve from the tip downwards and along the shadowed edge and where the closed petals overlap. Add more depth by dropping in a stronger mix of quinacridone magenta and indigo. Leave to dry.

Tip

Use two brushes, one for applying the paint and the other for glazing and diffusing colour with clean water.

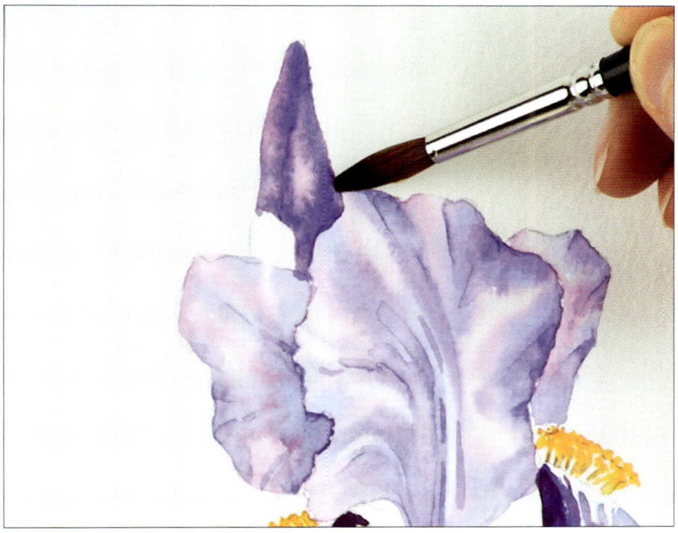

20 Repeat this technique for the other bud at the top of the flower, omitting the inital yellow-green colour.

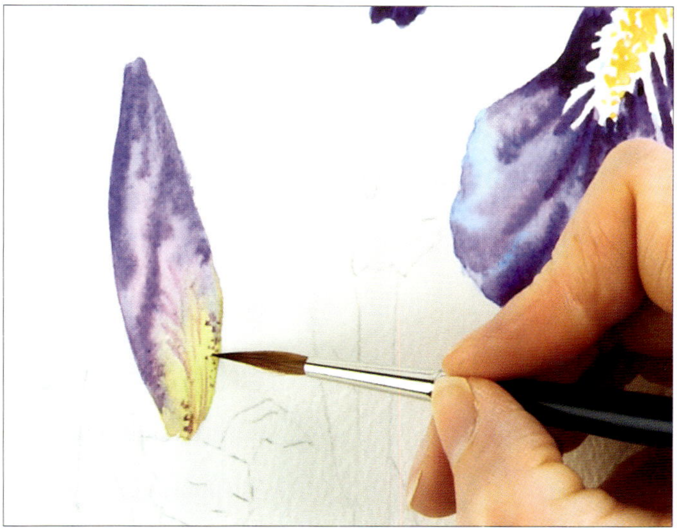

21 Using the pink-mauve and a size 5 round brush, indicate veining on the first, lower bud by stippling with the tip of your brush.

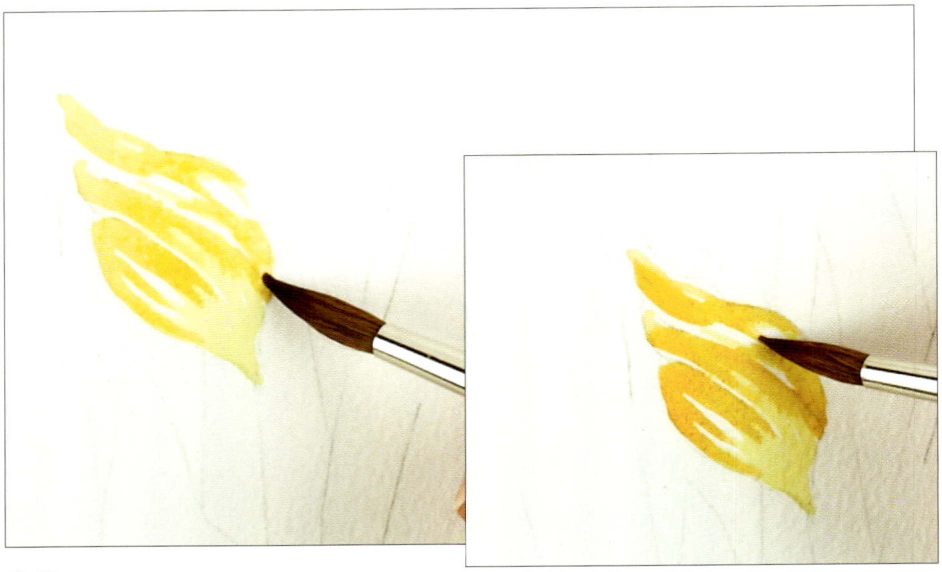

22 Change to a size 8 round brush and prepare a pale mix of aureolin with a touch of raw sienna, a dilute and a strong pool of raw sienna, and a mauve mix of quinacridone magenta and French ultramarine. Apply a wash of aureolin with raw sienna on the lower papery covering at the base of the stem. Draw the colour from the base upwards, leaving gaps of white. Draw raw sienna downwards to overlap the initial wash. While still damp, load your brush with the stronger mix of raw sienna and draw it downwards on the shaded side, stopping short of the previous brushstrokes.

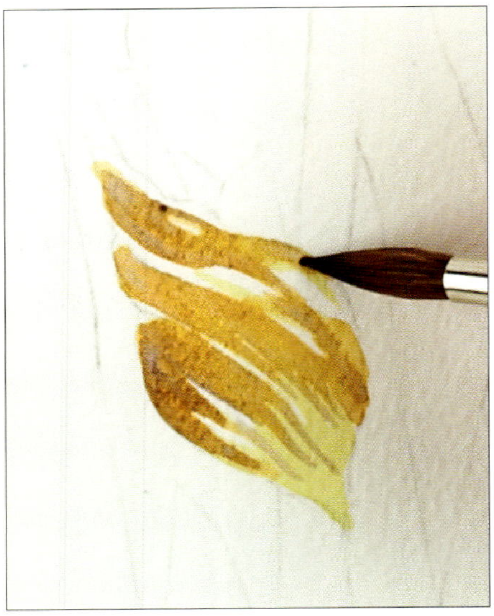

23 To add more depth on the shadowed side, apply a little of the mauve mix, allowing the colours to blend together. Leave to dry.

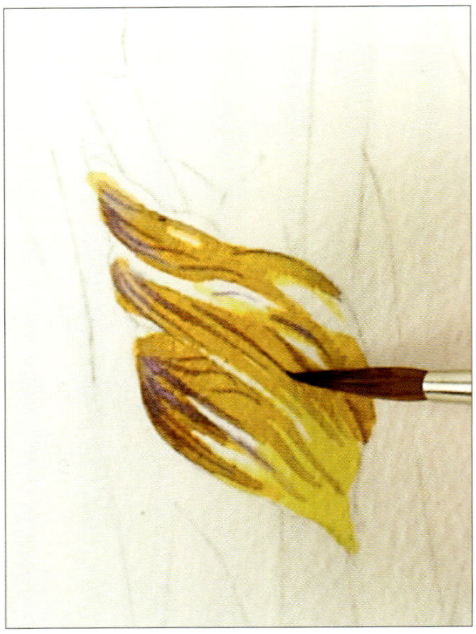

24 Load the size 5 round brush with the mauve mix and add in the veins. Draw the brush from the left side downwards with the point of the brush. Mauve and yellow are complementary colours which neutralise each other, so when the mauve is applied to the yellow base, it becomes a warm pink-brown, linking well with the overall painting.

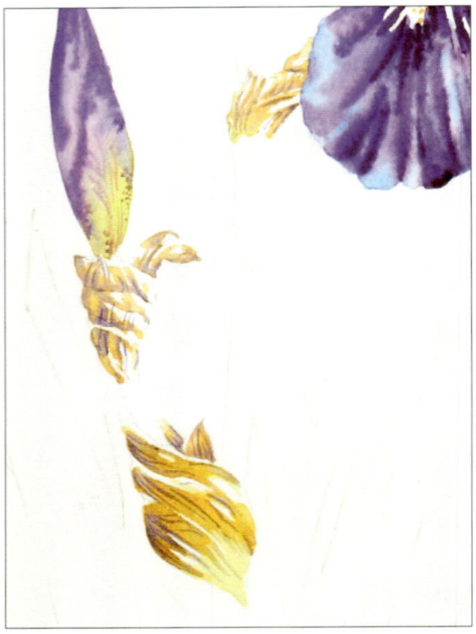

25 Continue to paint the remaining papery bud coverings in the same way. The veins follow the contours of the folds.

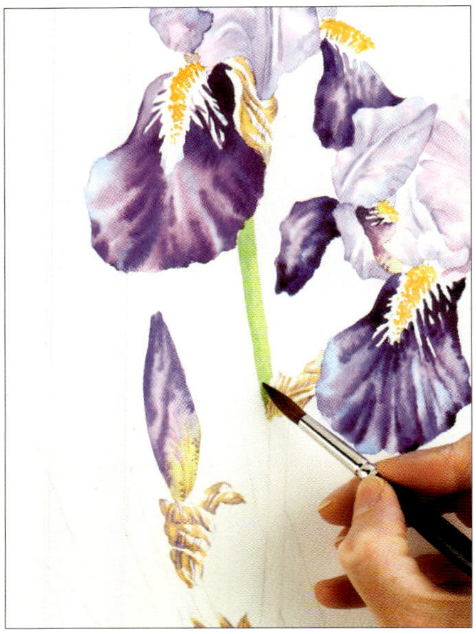

26 Return to the size 8 round brush and prepare two mixes: aureolin with a touch of French ultramarine to make a yellow-green and French ultramarine with a dash of aureolin for a blue-green. Apply a base wash of yellow-green on each section of the stem. Work from the top downwards.

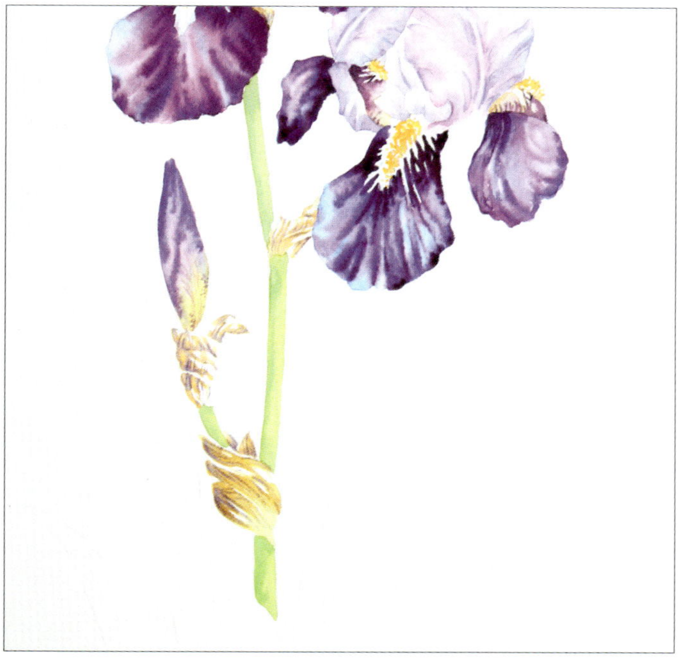

27 While still wet, run your brush loaded with the blue-green mix along the shaded left-hand side of the stem, to add depth and form.

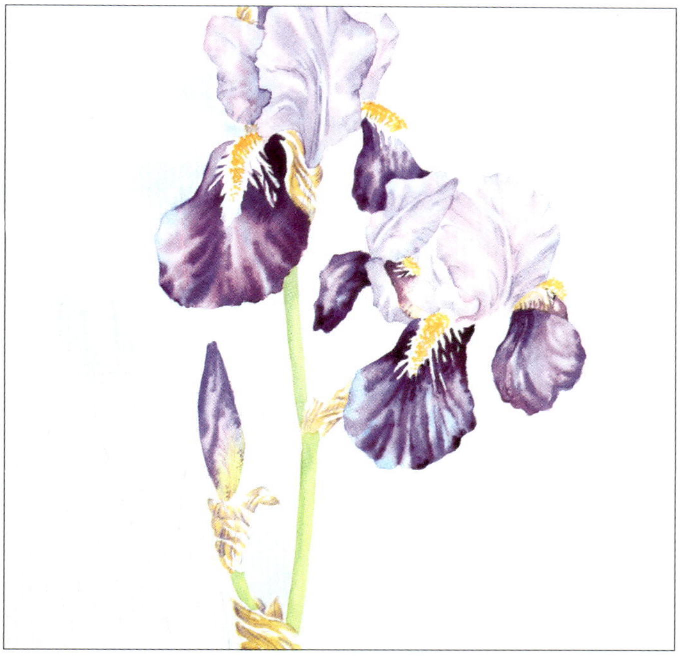

28 Mix two dilute pools of colour: French ultramarine and a mauve mix of quinacridone magenta with French ultramarine. Tilt your painting at an angle of approximately 30° and apply the background wash with a size 12 round brush. Commence with French ultramarine on the left-hand side of the stem. Carefully paint around the petals and stem and diffuse with clean water towards the base.

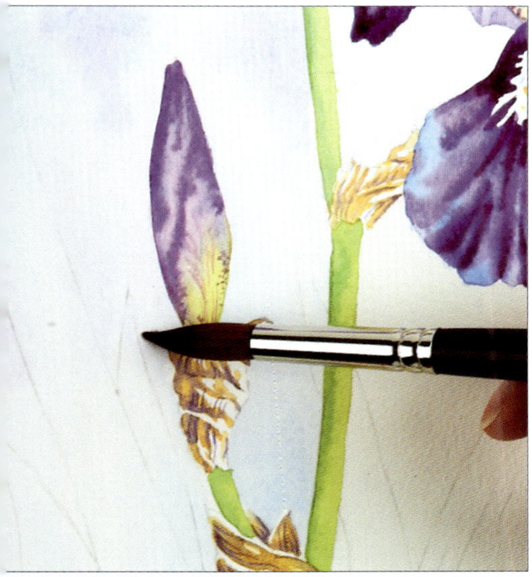

29 While still wet, drop in touches of mauve paint. Tilt the board back and forth to encourage the colours to blend. Repeat steps 28 and 29 on the right-hand side of the stem. Leave to dry.

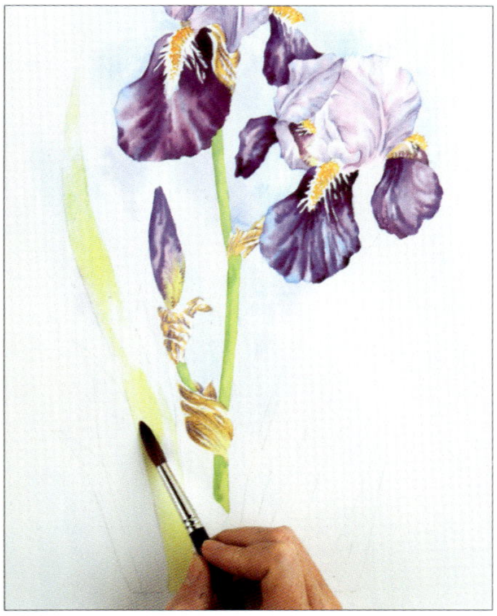

30 Prepare three pools of colour to create a variegated wash for the leaves: aureolin, cobalt blue and cerulean blue. Work on alternate leaves so that the colours do not run together. Glaze the tallest leaf with clean water using a size 12 brush and drop in patches of aureolin yellow with a size 10 brush.

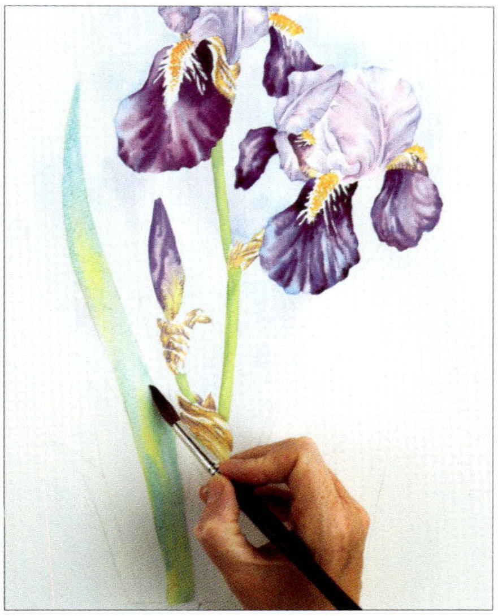

31 Load your brush with the cerulean blue. Starting at the tip of the wet leaf, draw the point of your brush downwards towards the base of the leaf. When the blue touches the yellow base wash, it will become a green shade.

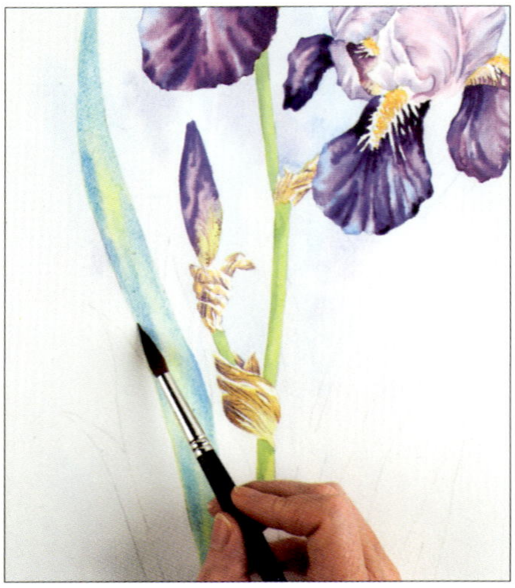

32 While the leaf is still damp, load your brush with cobalt blue and again draw the point of your brush down from the tip of the leaf to the base and along some of the edges. Continue painting the alternate leaves in the same way and leave to dry.

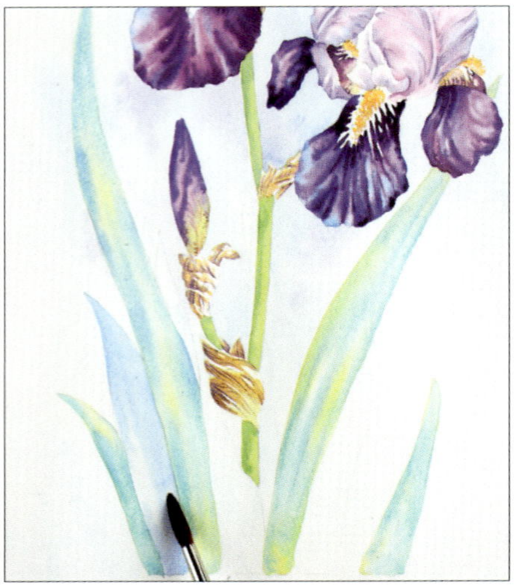

33 Paint in the remaining leaves. Glaze with clean water and apply the colours in a different sequence, commencing with cobalt blue.

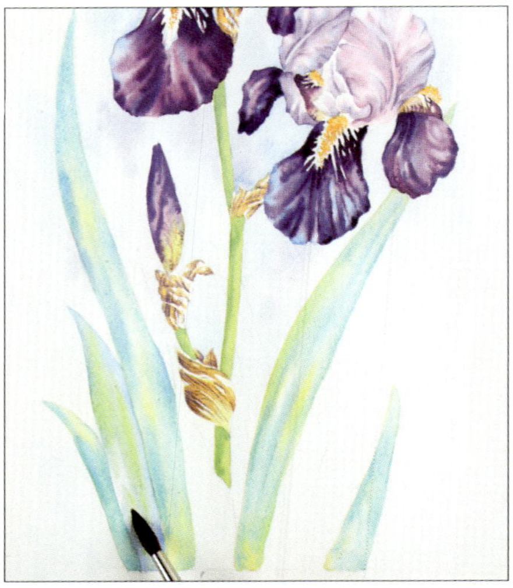

34 While wet, apply the aureolin in patches on top of the cobalt blue.

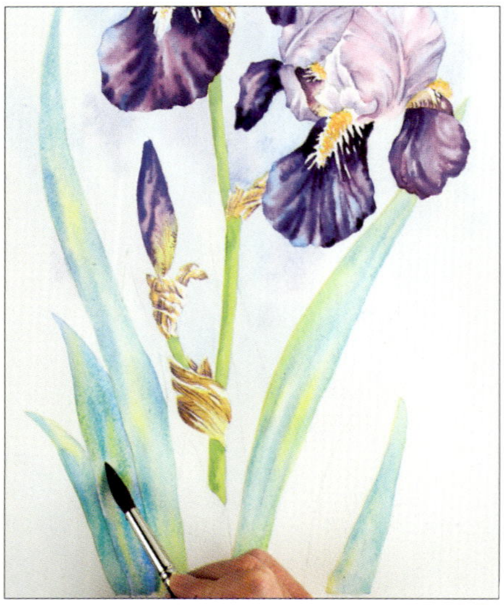

35 Finally apply cerulean blue in downward strokes, using the tip of your brush. Complete the rest of the leaves using the same colour sequence.

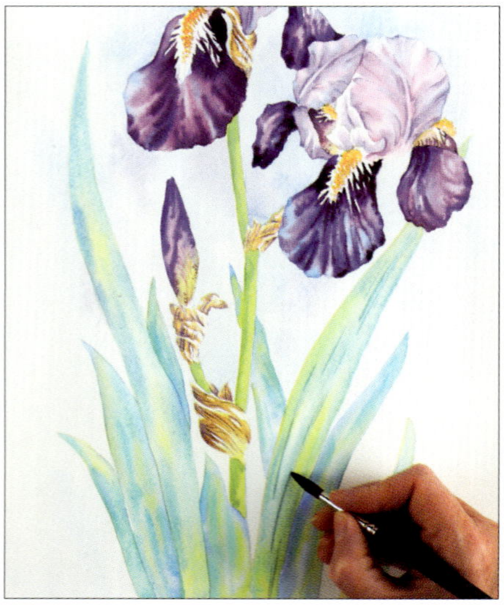

36 Change to a size 8 round brush and prepare a strong green made up of equal parts of French ultramarine and aureolin. Working from the base of each leaf and using the point of the brush, draw the paint upwards to suggest the veins.

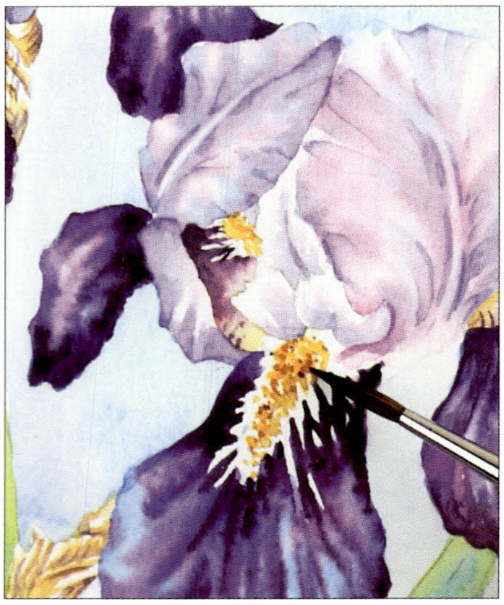

37 Balance the colour of the stamens by stippling in more strength of colour with a size 5 round brush. Use a pink-purple mix of quinacridone magenta with French ultramarine. When dry, remove all of the visible pencil lines with a clean eraser.

Tip

When adding in fine details such as veins, hold your brush lower down for greater control.

Opposite

The finished painting, reduced in size.

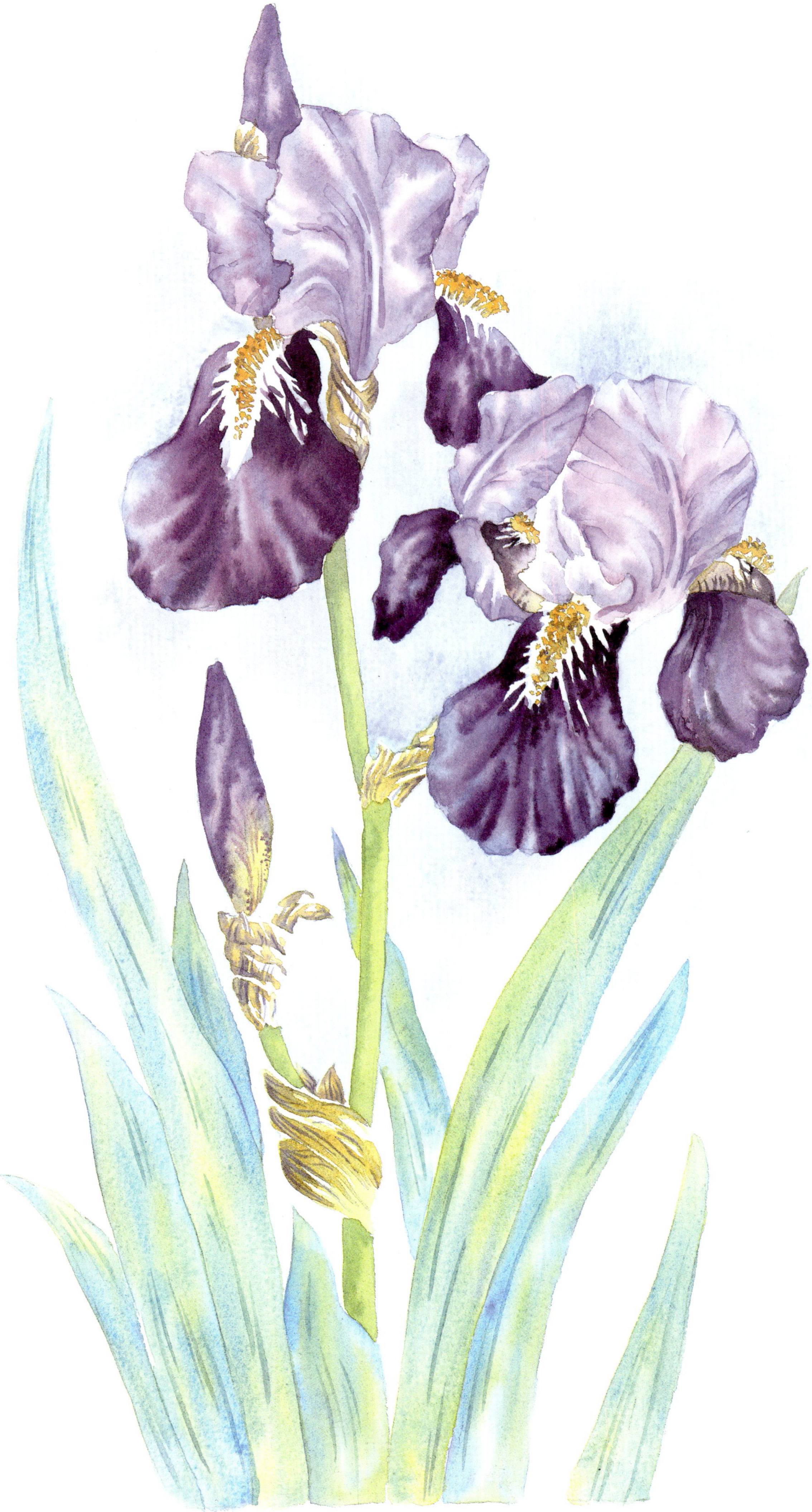

White Iris

TRACING 5

I love to visually zoom in to a flower head and cover my paper with one bloom. Leaving the iris shape as white paper, I worked on the variegated background using the wet-in-wet technnique and introduced negative painting to suggest the leaves. I retained plenty of white paper on the flower head and gave the petals movement by using sweeping brushstrokes.

You will need

300gsm (140lb) Not watercolour paper

Masking fluid

Colours: aureolin, new gamboge, Indian yellow, raw sienna, cobalt blue, French ultramarine, permanent rose, quinacridone magenta, sap green

Brushes: size 5 round, size 8 round, size 10 round, size 12 round, old brush

Pencils: 2B, H

Kitchen paper

Eraser

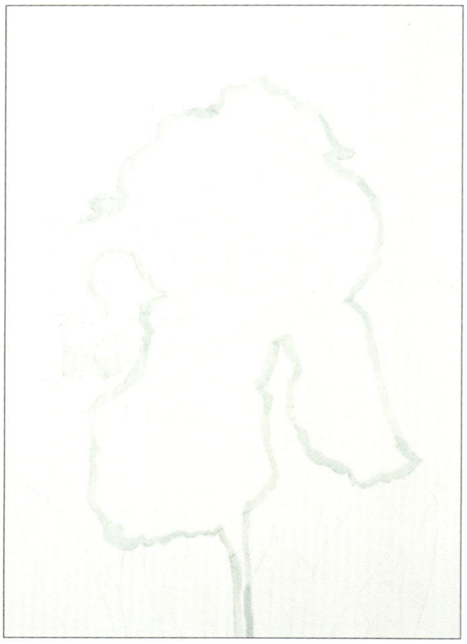

1 Transfer the tracing to your paper following the instructions on page 9. Using an old brush, paint a thick brushstroke along the inner edge of the pencil line of the flower head and stem with masking fluid. Rinse your brush in water with a little washing up liquid added. Allow to dry thoroughly. In preparation for working on the background wet-in-wet, tilt your board slightly so as to work at an angle.

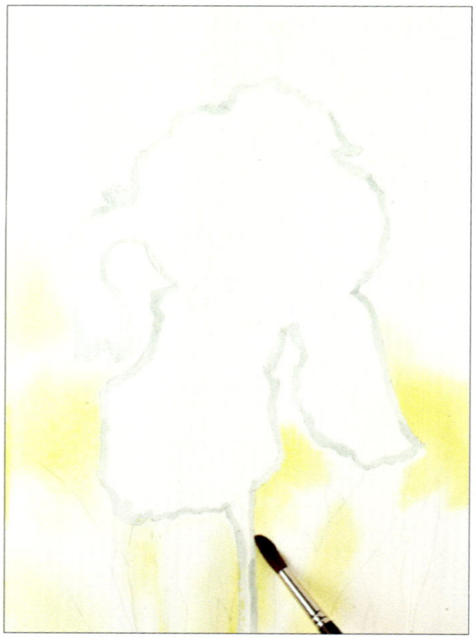

2 For the background, prepare the following large pools of colour: aureolin, cobalt blue, sap green and a mauve mix of quinacridone magenta and a touch of cobalt blue. Glaze the background with water using a size 12 round brush or any alternative large brush. To check that you have wet your paper sufficiently, view it from an angle so that you can see a shine on the surface. Using a size 10 round brush, apply aureolin in patches towards the base of the picture.

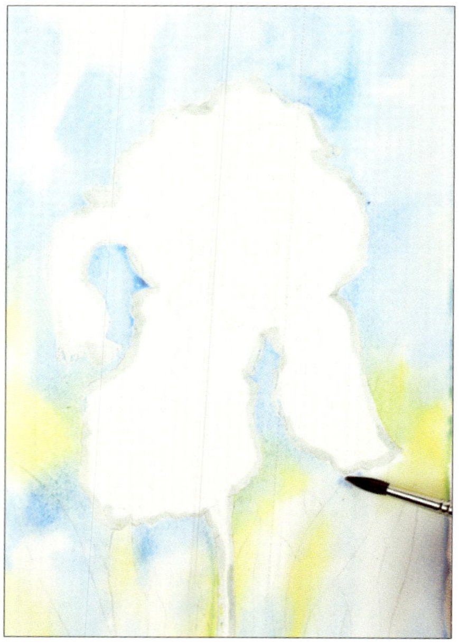

3 Load your brush with the cobalt blue and apply in patches, adding more blue towards the top of the picture. When the colours meet, they will create a green shade.

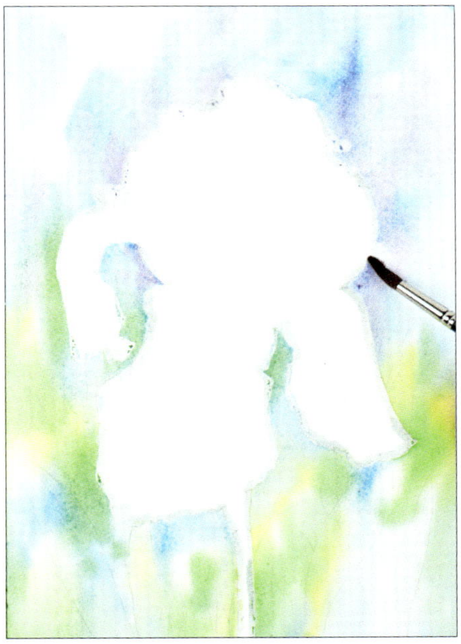

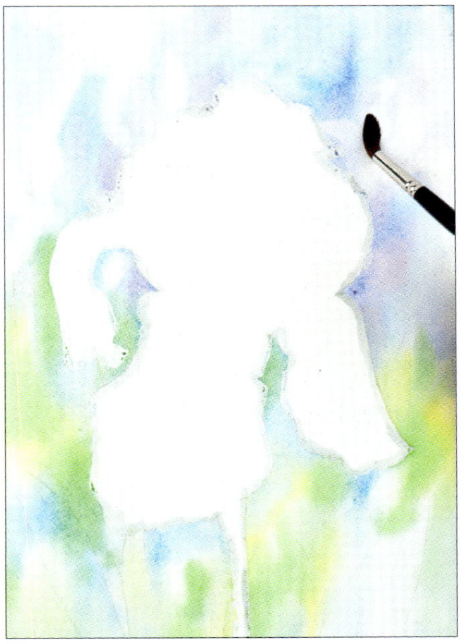

4 Working quickly, drop in sap green towards the bottom of the picture to establish the basis for the foreground leaves. Tip the board in different directions to allow the colours to blend.

5 Load your brush with the mauve mix and drop the colour in towards the top half of the picture. Tip the board to blend and diffuse the colour.

6 When the paint has dried slightly, lift some colour out of the background by rolling a brush, dipped in clean water, over the paint. Dab the paint you lift out on to a piece of kitchen paper. This technique will give the impression that other irises are present in the far background.

Tip

If you find you have any puddles of excess colour sitting on the surface on the paper, lift it out by dabbing with a dry brush.

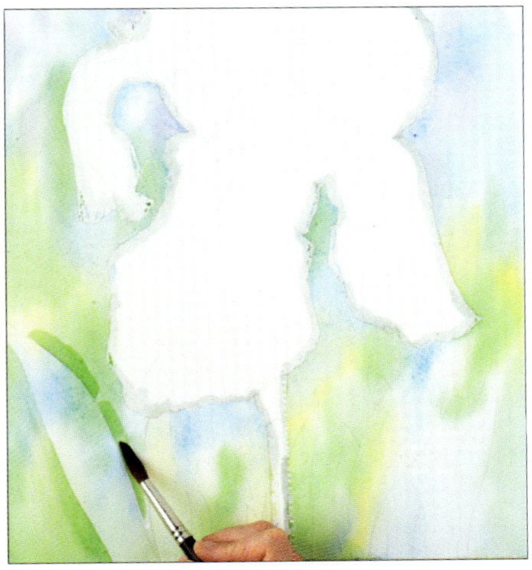

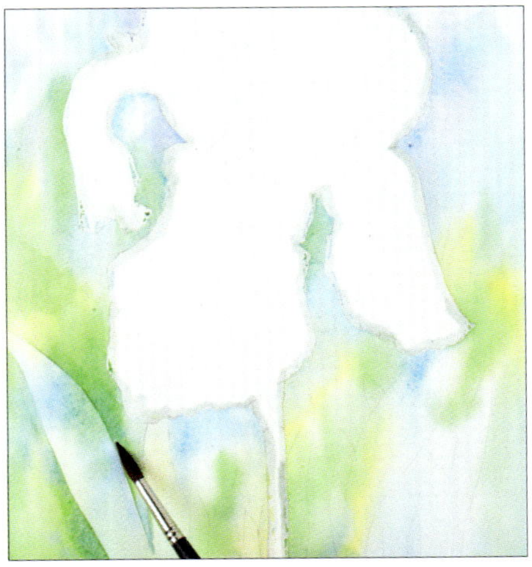

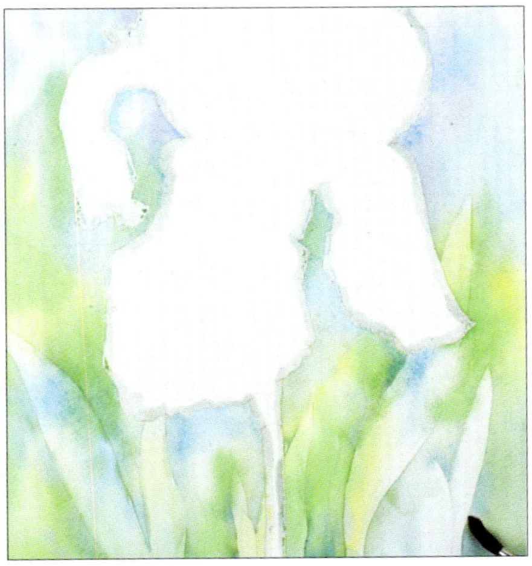

7 Continuing with the size 10 round brush, prepare a green mix of French ultramarine with aureolin for the negative painting stage. Working wet-on-dry, paint in a brushstroke surrounding the lower left-hand leaf. Quickly dip your brush in water and diffuse the colour. Keep adding water until no hard edges can be seen.

8 Diffuse the colour on the other outside edge. While the paper is still damp, drop in cobalt blue to give a variegated colour effect. While still a little damp, soften a few hard edges between the leaf margin and background with a damp brush. Paint in the rest of the leaves using this technique. Leave to dry.

9 Using a stronger blue-green mix of French ultramarine and aureolin, add more depth to the areas surrounding the leaves, again working wet-on-dry, diffusing with water.

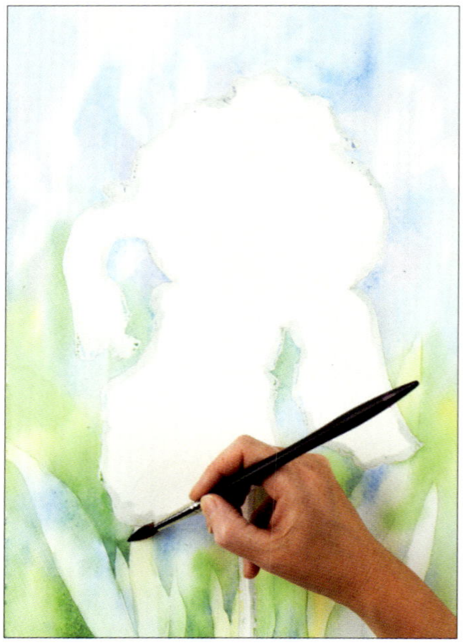

10 Continue deepening the colour around the leaves, working from left to right. Where one leaf overlaps, paint a wash of colour on the leaf further back, again softening the edge. Leave to dry.

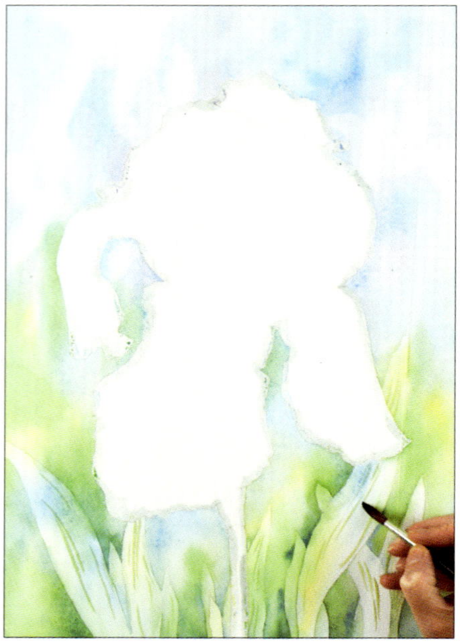

11 Change to a size 8 round brush and draw in a few veins using the paler mix of green. Work from the base of each leaf upwards.

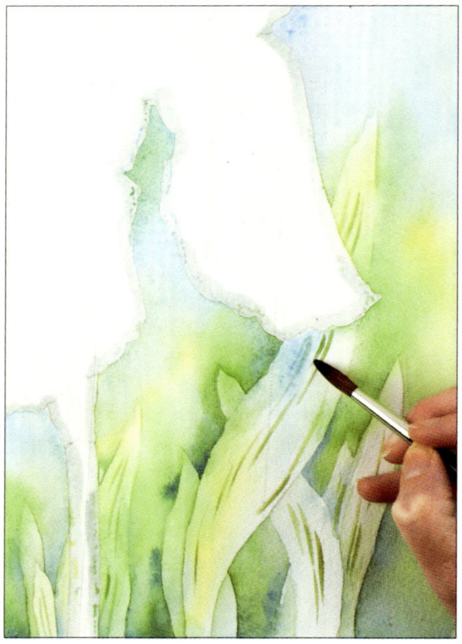

12 Using a slightly stronger mix of the two colours, add more depth on the veins by adding in a brushstroke here and there. Leave to dry.

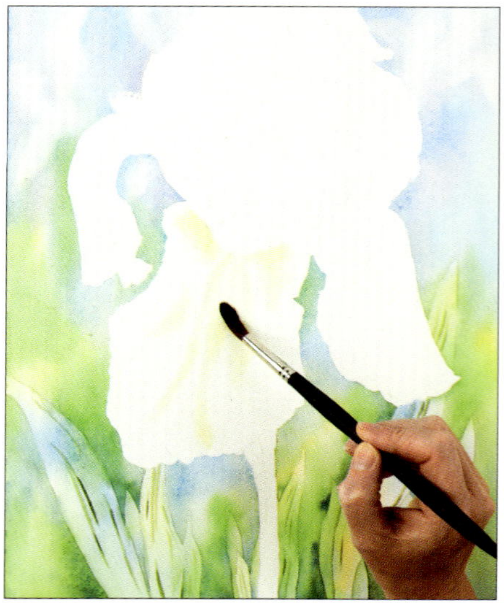

13 When the paper is throughly dry, rub off the masking fluid with an eraser or with your finger. Change to a size 12 round brush and loosely wet the lower petal with water. Change to a size 10 round brush and apply aureolin from the top curved edge, drawing lightly downwards to add form.

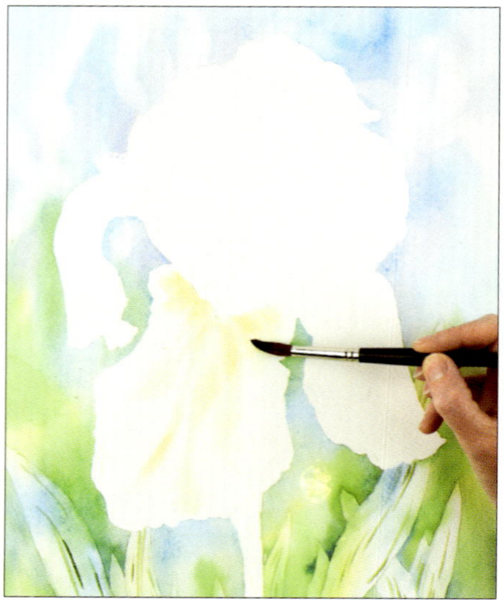

14 Add in some touches of raw sienna whilst still damp, sweeping your brushstrokes downwards to follow the curve of the petal.

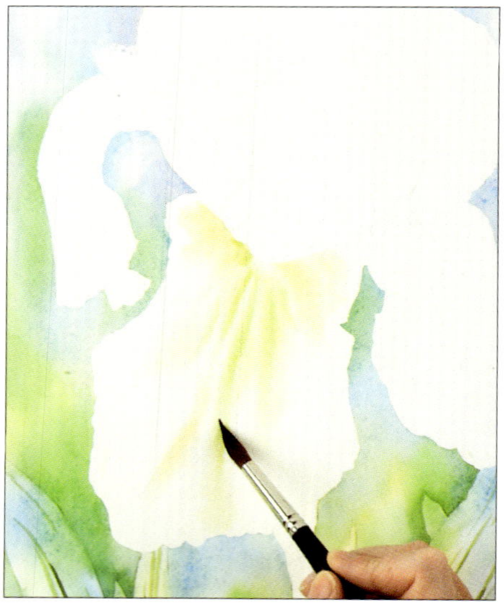

15 Prepare a mix of sap green and a touch of new gamboge to make a fresh green colour. Again, working on slightly damp paper, draw a few light brushstrokes downwards. Leave to dry.

Tip

When you make new colour mixes, don't worry if you are unable to reach the same colour as you had before. The variation in colour will add to the natural look of the painting.

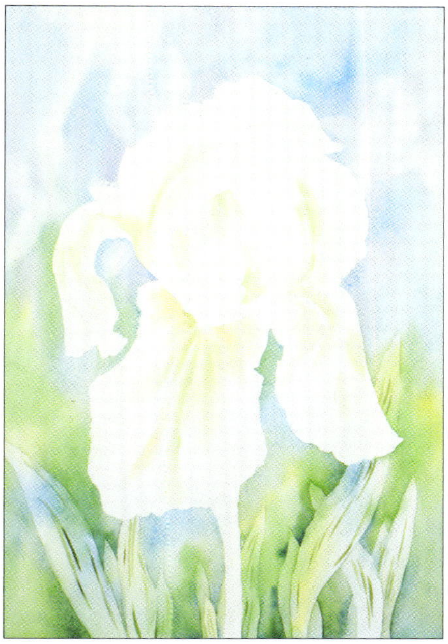

16 Glaze each of the other petals with water and repeat the process of applying aureolin, followed by raw sienna and the fresh green. Apply less on the top petals and work the brushstrokes from the base upwards to suggest the curve of the central vein.

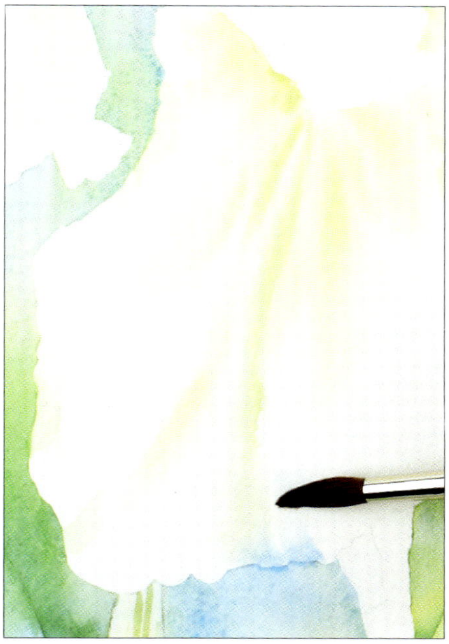

17 Connect some of the background colour to the petal edges by applying a few soft touches of sap green and cobalt blue. This will make the edges appear less hard and stark.

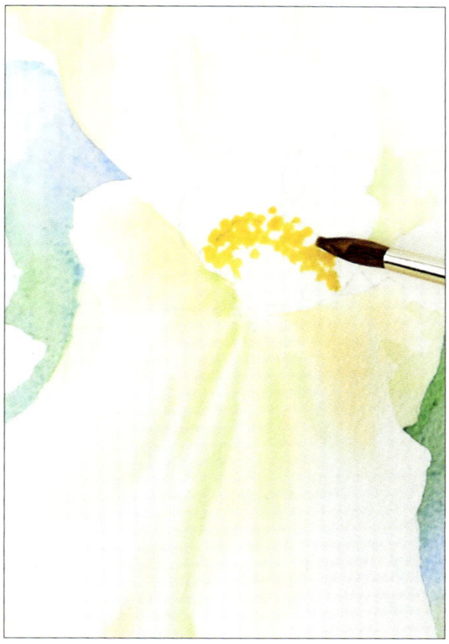

18 Prepare a pool of aureolin and a pool of new gamboge. Change to a size 8 round brush and, with the point of the brush, stipple in the base colour of the stamens using the cool aureolin mix. Whilst still damp, stipple on top with new gamboge.

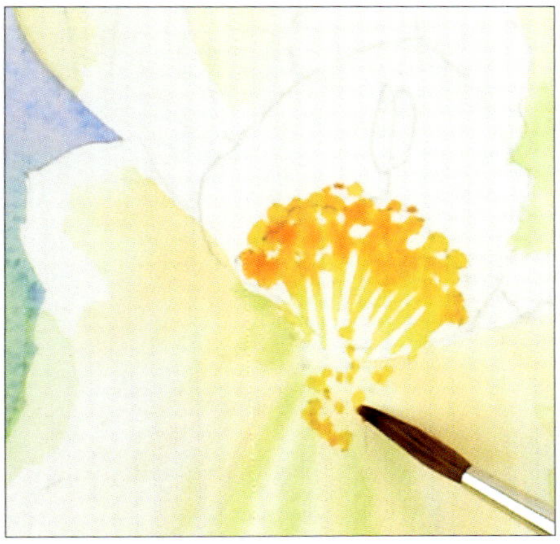

19 Change to a size 5 round brush and prepare a mix of aureolin with a dash of cobalt blue. Draw fine brushstrokes downwards from the stippled area, allowing the colours to merge. While still damp, increase the strength of the stamens by dropping in Indian yellow and stipple a few extra dots of yellow on the petal beneath. Paint in the other stamen using the same technique as described in steps 18 and 19.

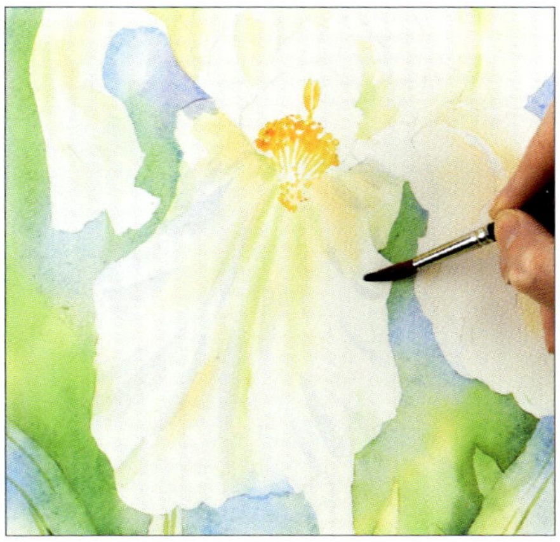

20 Mix a pale shade of grey: cobalt blue plus permanent rose with a tiny touch of raw sienna. Return to the size 8 brush and apply sweeping brushstrokes wet-on-dry. Work from the edge of the petal inwards and along the centre to suggest the shadowed recesses of the petal folds. Leave plenty of white paper. Continue painting in the remaining petals in the same way. Leave to dry.

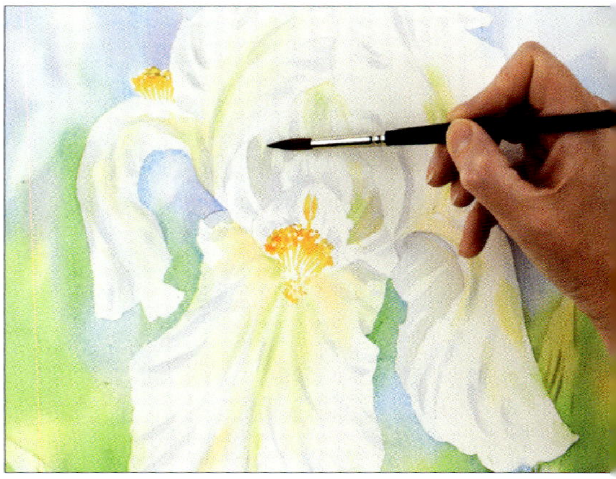

21 Mix a stronger shade of the grey using the same colours. Apply the colour into all the areas of shadow in the centre of the flower. Paint sweeping brushstrokes on top of, or close to, the existing pale grey brushstrokes on all the petals. Leave to dry.

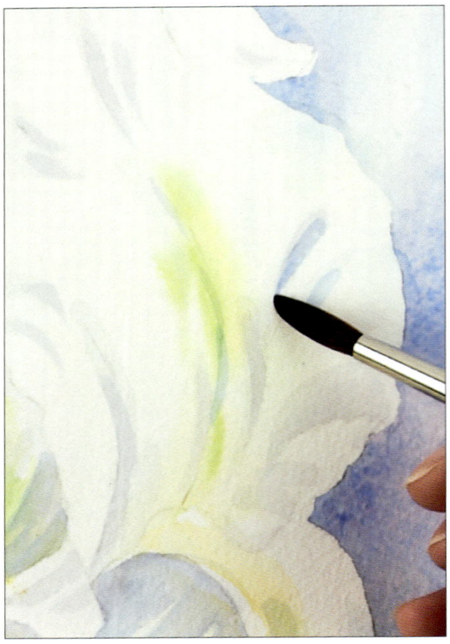

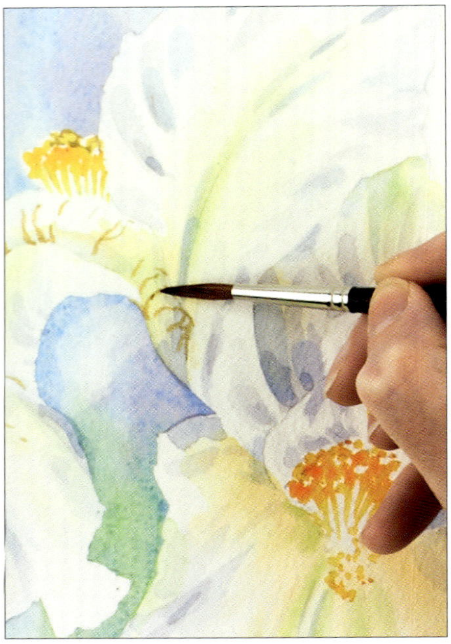

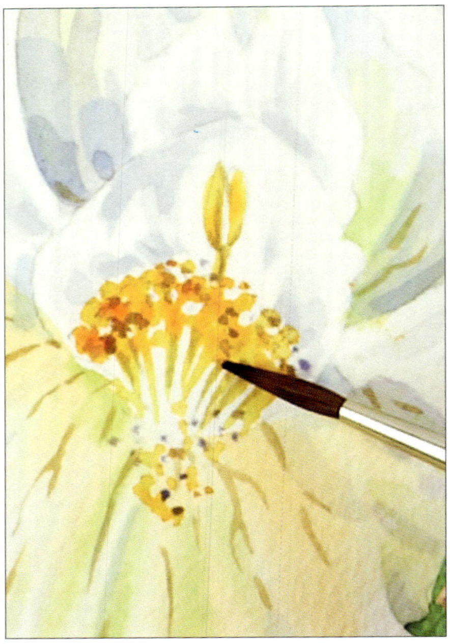

22 White petals reflect their surroundings so in order to add more depth and life, add a few light, shorter brushstrokes of dilute cobalt blue on top of some of the existing grey brushstrokes.

23 Change to a size 5 round brush and prepare a green-brown shade: raw sienna plus a small amount of French ultramarine. Paint in the fine details such as the veins on the far left-hand petal, which is slightly curled under, and the filaments supporting the stamen.

24 Prepare a strong pink-mauve mix of permanent rose and cobalt blue, and using the point of your brush, stipple this colour on to the stamens to add interest on top of the yellow tones. Paint in the stigma on the central flower head using new gamboge followed by Indian yellow, and strengthen with the pink-mauve.

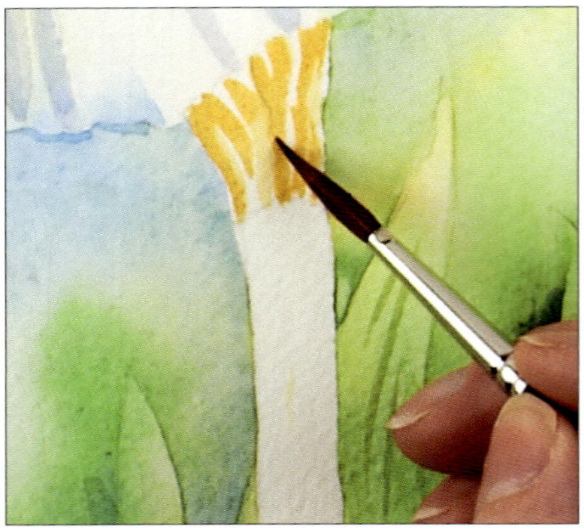

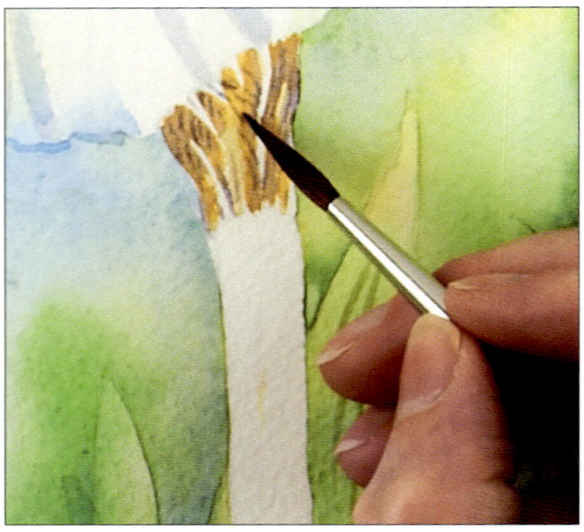

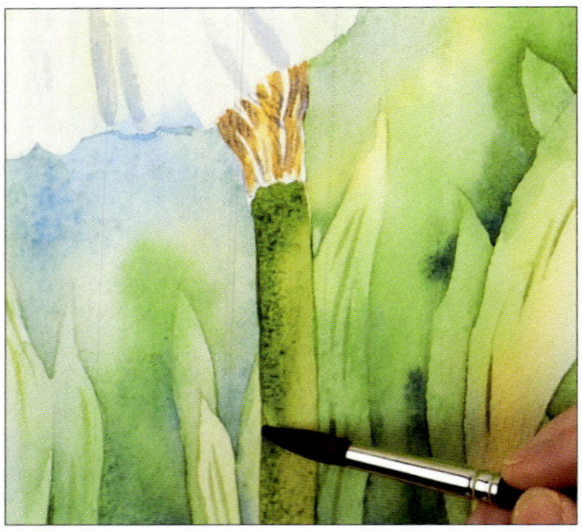

25 For the papery covering on the stem, paint in a base of raw sienna, leaving gaps of white to describe its crinkly texture. While still wet, go over the lines on the papery covering with a stronger shade of raw sienna.

26 While still damp, apply the mix of permanent rose and cobalt blue. Draw the point of the brush downwards, allowing the colours to blend. Leave to dry.

27 Change to a size 8 round brush and apply a mid-tone shade of green using French ultramarine and aureolin, working from the top to the base of the stem. Strengthen the mix and, while the base is still wet, run your brush along the left-hand shaded side. Leave to dry and remove any visible pencil lines with an eraser.

Opposite

The finished painting.

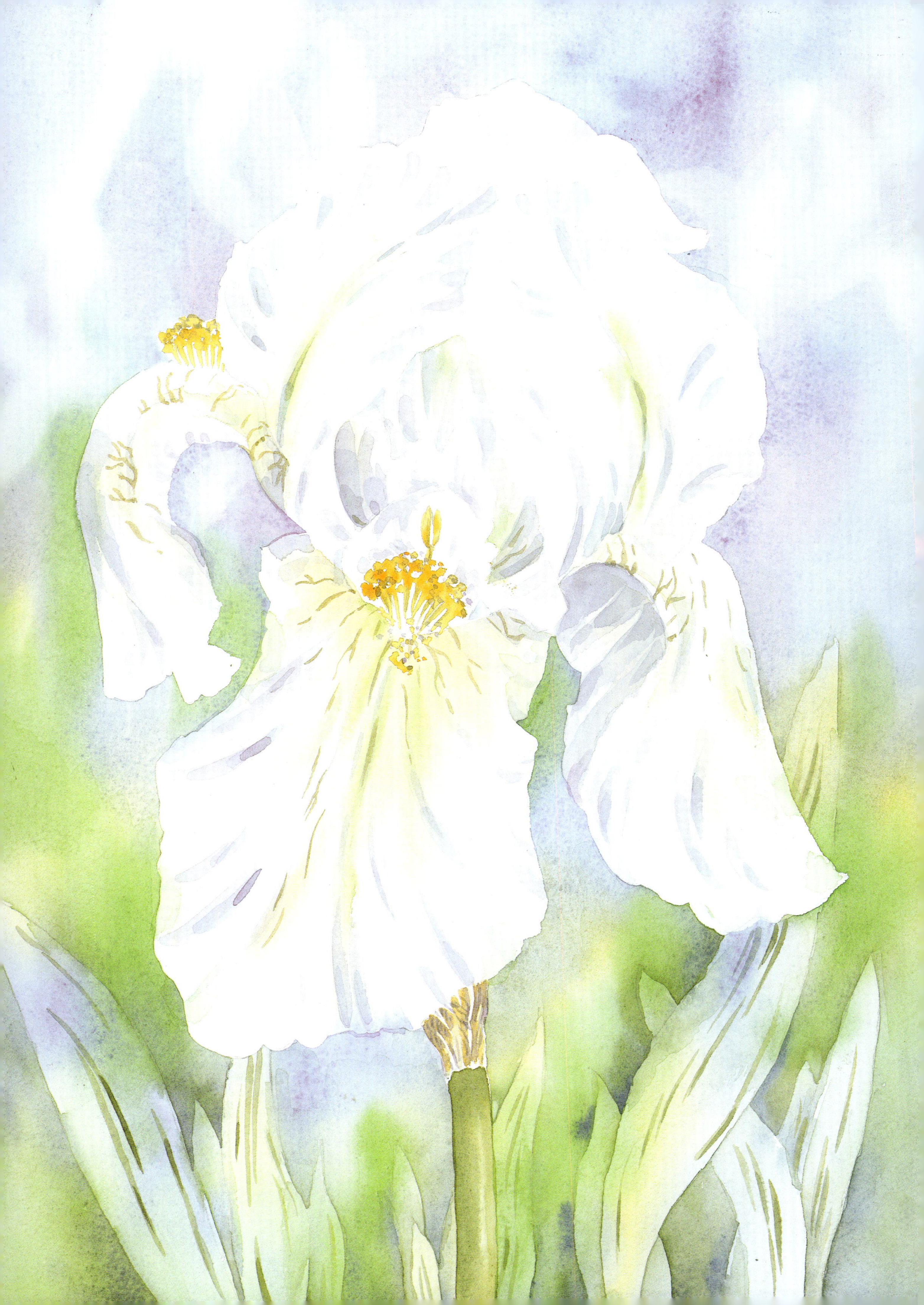

Index

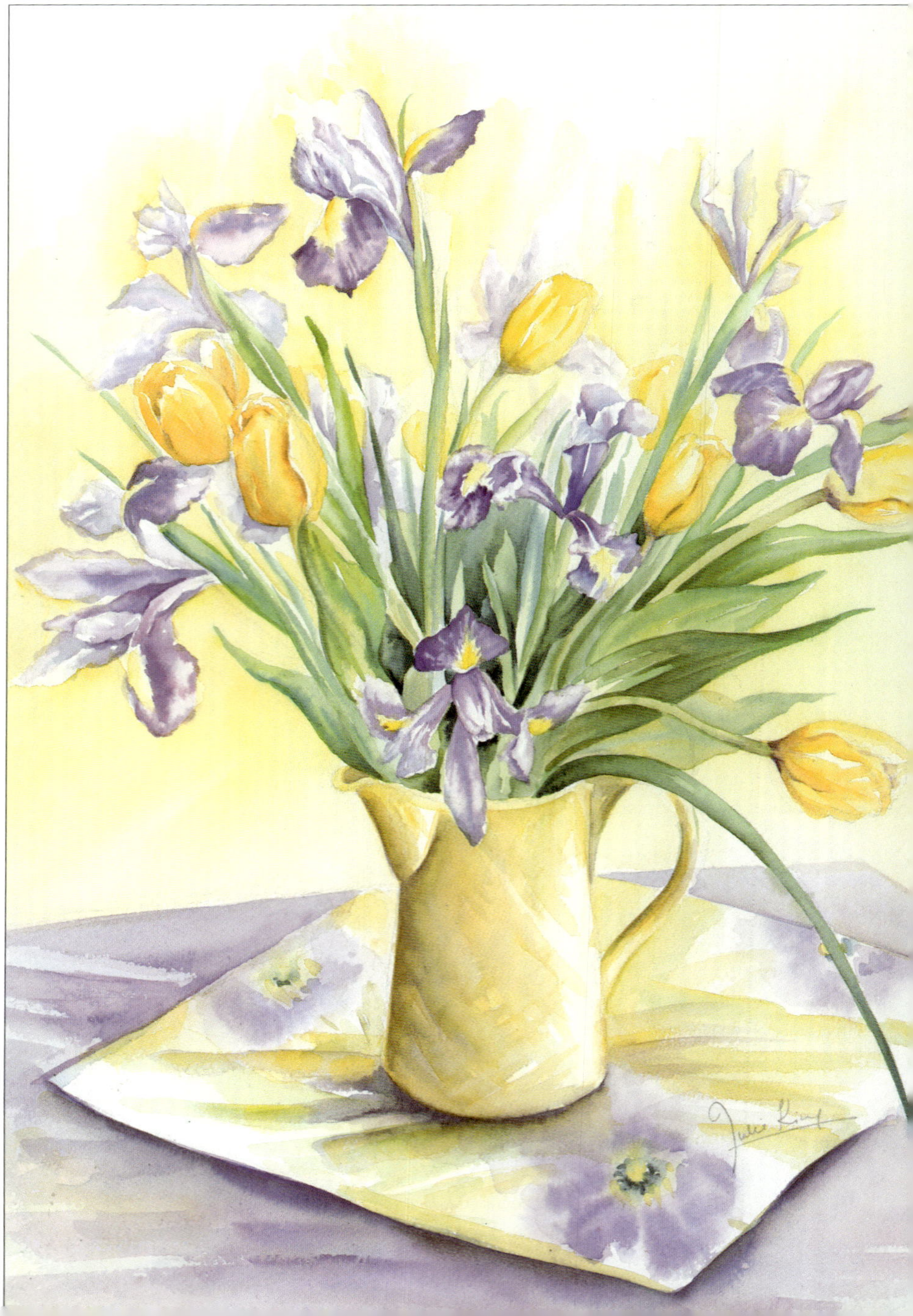

The Yellow Jug

30.5 x 41.5cm (12 x 16½in)

I have used the contrasting colours and shapes of mauve irises and yellow tulips to create a fresh and vibrant painting. The yellow of the tulips is echoed in the background and the mauve of the irises in the cloth, giving a balanced composition.